The Happiness Paradox

Focus on Contemporary Issues (FOCI) addresses the pressing problems, ideas and debates of the new millennium. Subjects are drawn from the arts, sciences and humanities, and are linked by the impact they have had or are having on contemporary culture. FOCI books are intended for an intelligent, alert audience with a general understanding of, and curiosity about, the intellectual debates shaping culture today. Instead of easing readers into a comfortable awareness of particular fields, these books are combative. They offer points of view, take sides and are written with passion.

SERIES EDITORS
Barrie Bullen and Peter Hamilton

In the same series

The Happiness Paradox

ZIYAD MARAR

REAKTION BOOKS

For Kate and our daughters

Published by Reaktion Books Ltd
79 Farringdon Road
London EC1M 3JU, UK

www.reaktionbooks.co.uk

First published 2003

Series design by Libanus Press
Printed and bound in Great Britain by
Cromwell Press, Trowbridge, Wiltshire

British Library Cataloguing in Publishing Data
Marar, Ziyad
   The happiness paradox. – (FOCI)
   1. Happiness
   I. Title
   152.4'2

ISBN 1 86189 182 2

Contents

Introduction

On a recent visit to Amman (my father is Jordanian), I asked one of my uncles whether he was happy. He talked for a while about his work, his family, their health, my grandfather, the state of the economy. I pressed for more: 'But are you actually *happy*?' After a while he just looked at me blankly. It became clear to me that I had made a *category mistake*, like the first-time visitor to Oxford who asked Gilbert Ryle after being shown a collection of colleges, libraries, playing fields, museums, scientific departments and administrative buildings, 'But where is the university?' For my uncle, this peculiarly Western question was incoherent when detached from the aspects of life that contribute to a good life, well-lived.

So why take on the task of writing about happiness? Happiness 'writes white', as poets like to say. Tolstoy opened *Anna Karenina* with a similar thought: 'All happy families are alike, each unhappy family is unhappy in its own way.'[1] Indeed, the term *happy* is so dull and ubiquitous that it has been worn thin; rubbed transparent through constant, casual usage: as long as they're happy, whatever makes you happy, I'm happy to do that, happy as Larry, happy hunting ground, happy hour, happy go lucky, happy endings and happily ever after. The term is a mindless refrain for those who give up on thinking. It is anodyne, the limit point of banality. Aldous Huxley once commented that he could 'sympathize with people's pains, but not with their pleasures. There is something curiously boring about somebody else's happiness.'[2]

Some would say that only the stupid could be happy in such a complex, unhappy world. Coco Chanel in an interview captures the tone: 'You ask if they were happy. This is not a characteristic of a European. To be contented – that's for the cows.'[3] The very idea seems untextured, toothless, 'happy clappy'. The concept belongs in some virginal fairyland, bleached of nuance and subtlety. The terrain of real life, criss-crossed by pain and beauty and smells and tears and dignity and ideas and eroticism, simply cannot have its contours reflected by such a shapeless notion. Better to side with J. S. Mill in preferring to be a miserable Socrates than a happy pig. The idea doesn't make for good conversation – after all, what is less interesting than a happy childhood? This is why Bertrand Russell once observed that 'Men who are unhappy, like men who sleep badly, are always proud of the fact.'

And yet, there is something irresistible about this vanilla conceit. We applaud Philip Larkin's wish for the new-born Sally Amis:

. . . may you be dull –
If that is what a skilled,
Vigilant, flexible,
Unemphasised, enthralled
Catching of happiness is called.[4]

We crave happiness even if we can't define it, and even as we resist being defined by it. It represents the all-purpose opposite of . . . well, unhappiness. Unhappiness has none of the banality of its opposite, it is deadly serious – the land of pain, fear, grief, rejection, shame, terror, fury, sorrow. If only in running from unhappiness we run towards happiness. Everything we claim to desire is pursued as a means to that end; rivers running into the sea. The philosopher George Santayana once observed that 'Happiness is the only sanction of life; where happiness fails, existence remains a mad and lamentable experiment.'[5] It is the only good answer to the question *What would you ask for if you had only one wish?* It is the thing we want for our children.

We are also aware of the fact that many (maybe most) people who are privileged enough to enjoy physical comforts, work, health and political freedom are restlessly striving for happiness, but rarely find it. They are mystified, if not tormented, by fleeting wisps that vanish before they can be recognized. Too often they are left confused, sad, alone in their 'lives of quiet desperation' (in Henry David Thoreau's evocative phrase).

The Happiness Paradox does not attempt to offer therapy, or practical advice on how to live a happy life. Rather, this book is an attempt to understand the idea of happiness, to explore what others have said about it, and to try to clarify what is at stake in its pursuit. Above all, I want to explain its elusiveness.

The Modern Malaise

It has become commonplace to reflect on the fact that Western societies have broken away from many of the old certainties. The contemporary emphasis on the internet, fast food culture, MTV life styles, flexible working patterns are but the most vivid markers of a massive shift in the way we view our culture and ourselves. The postmodernist credo – heralding the death of authors, meta-narratives, foundations, truths, rationality, the subject, morality and other examples of what the philosopher Hilary Putnam calls 'God's eye points of view' – is a theoretical blade that has cut us loose from the bonds of certainty and left a question-mark in its place. We recognize that this blade is double-edged: that while liberation from old structures and beliefs has freed us from the constraints of 'knowing our place', we have simultaneously discarded the moral frameworks that underpinned our experience and provided a sense of direction. In breaking free to dream of new possibilities, we have traded in our organizing principles and have killed off certainty.

The question for our age is, once we have achieved this freedom from old-fashioned constraints, what do we do with it? In many ways our expectations are being raised while our tools for delivering on those expectations are increasingly impoverished. Walter Lippman in *Drift and Mastery* spoke eloquently at the beginning of the twentieth century of a spirit that even more strongly defines than the cultural climate of the twenty-first:

> We are unsettled to the very roots of our being . . . the loss of something outside ourselves which we can obey is a revolutionary break with our habits. Never before have we had to rely so completely upon ourselves. No guardians to think for us, no precedent to follow without question, no lawmaker above, only ordinary men set to deal with heart-breaking perplexity. Of course, our culture is confused, our thinking spasmodic, and our emotion out of kilter. No mariner enters upon a more uncharted sea than does the average human being born into the 20th century. Our ancestors thought they knew their way from birth through all eternity: we are puzzled about the day after tomorrow . . . .[6]

Lippman offered science and rationalism as a way out of the problem. Nearly a century, and many wars, later, even science is greeted with the same scepticism as previous sources of authority, and can no longer offer that comfort. This trend has only accelerated, and since the liberation culture of the 1960s has reached ever purer expression. This is not to say we all live in an amoral sink, just that traditional sources of morality are not what they used to be. The particular shape of this contemporary problem is reflected in the kinds of reasons for which people nowadays seek out therapy. E. H. Erikson noted that whereas

> the patient of early psychoanalysis suffered most under inhibitions which prevented him from being what and who he thought he was. [The contemporary patient] suffers most under the problem of what he should believe in and – or indeed might – be or become . . . [he suffers from] feelings of meaninglessness, feelings of emptiness, pervasive depression, lack of sustaining interests, goals, ideals and values, and 'feelings of unrelatedness' caused by 'the lack of ideologies and values' and the 'atmosphere of disillusionment and cynicism' in the surrounding society.[7]

No wonder people today find true happiness elusive! Many commentators fantasize about a return to simpler and more reliable codes. While they may be right to warn us against worshipping our new-found liberty alone, it is no solution to look for comfort in the past. Basking in rose-tinted nostalgia is a traditional response to the shock of the new, but as Lippman put it, 'people who are forever dreaming of a mythical past are merely saying they are afraid of the future'.

Our culture is shot through both by the dazzling dream of new horizons and self-expression, as well as the lowering shadow of responsibility and accountability. Happiness has become a necessary aspiration for an acceptable way of life. This questing impulse is today found in the rise of back-packers combing the lonely planet, or people who sit at the feet of yogis looking for inner peace, or the exhausting search for the body beautiful. Our politicians now embody the public requirement that we place happiness as our overarching purpose. Tony Blair and Bill Clinton, in his day, could not be seen without their ubiquitous grins (except of course when they were crying). Like Reagan before them they have understood that the job description of a political leader has changed from patriarchal moralist to the bloke next door who knows how to have a good time. Many have attributed Al Gore's failure, in the last US presidential election, to beat George W. Bush to just this factor.

The tormenting dream of happiness is a recent, and possibly local, but certainly irreversible invention, as I argue in chapter One. Harking back to happier and simpler times or fantasizing about collectivist societies are not answers to a pervasive contemporary problem. A contemporary assessment is needed.

At the heart of the modern question *Am I happy?* lie two further questions, namely *What do I really want?* and *How ought I to live?* The first is a recent question, the second is ancient. Together they pose a dilemma. Typically, the first question focuses on the internal search for our 'true self', and the second looks outward on the moral standards to which we can appeal in guiding our interactions with the world. This traditional framing of these two questions has left people stranded. Neither the self nor external standards have the solidity they once did. These questions seem incredibly hard to answer today, the one contradicts the other, and yet they are a central preoccupation in contemporary Western society. This paradoxical quality has its own history and character, which I will trace in this book. I will look at each of these questions in detail, while resisting the traditional assumptions about what underlies them. Under the headings freedom and justification, I will offer a different way of addressing them that better fits our modern self-image, and claim the tension between these two needs has a flip side that shows them to be mutually reinforcing. I will also explore how their paradoxical quality colours our experience of what Freud called the two central ingredients of a happy life: love and work.

Obviously, any attempt to talk about happiness needs to be heavily qualified. Happiness as discussed in this book can seem a rather privileged preoccupation. There are far larger forces that can shatter our chances of even a satisfactory existence. Everything from neuro-chemical imbalances to political oppression, from ill-health to major trauma can make the unhappiness that interests me trivial or irrelevant. And yet it seems to me undeniable that there are large numbers of people who have health, work, physical comforts or luxuries and who are still miserable, or simply baffled. More generally, while larger forces – biology on one side, society on the other – are at work shaping us in countless ways, they will not be central to my account of social and personal identity. My interest centres on our sense of self and how we are riven by conflict. Politics and genetics, for example, will only appear on the fringes of this text. More to the point, I think a preoccupation with happiness is of our time and place. The current obsession with the question *What do I really want?* poses a challenge to *How ought I to live?* at a time when many social structures and deities are losing their persuasive power. In a culture of millennial stocktaking, the paradox of happiness has never been so sharply in focus.

CHAPTER ONE

Happiness: A Brief History

There is that in me – I do not know what it is – but I know it is in me.

[. . .] I do not know it – it is without name – it is a word unsaid,
It is not in any dictionary, utterance, symbol.

Something it swings on more than the earth I swing on,
To it the creation is the friend whose embracing awakes me.

Do you see O my brothers and sisters?
It is not chaos or death – it is form, union, plan – it is eternal life – it is
Happiness.
Walt Whitman [1]

It is very hard to get a straight answer from people about what truly makes them happy. Psychologist Jonathan Freedman, working on his book *Happy People*, complained of a difficulty encountered by his research assistant in asking people this question. When she interviewed them in groups they joked and trivialized the idea, and when she interviewed them alone they became more serious, but stopped talking. She concluded they would rather talk about their sex lives than how happy they really were.[2]

Happiness is a deceptively simple term, yet remarkably elastic and hard to define. The *Oxford English Dictionary* traces its etymology to the same stem as *happen*, and *happenstance*, being what comes by luck or chance (as in a happy coincidence). Most dictionaries define happiness as a state of well-being and contentment. Beyond this, in everyday usage, we use a spill of overlapping terms such as high self-esteem, excitement, joy, contentment, pleasure, jubilation, serenity, ecstasy, satisfaction, cheerfulness, bliss and many more, to capture the sense of the word. Yet none of these words equates entirely with the feeling of happiness, despite the fact they all seem to bear on it strongly. 'Happiness' has many family resemblances but no synonyms.

So what makes us happy? Is it a sunny morning, a warm pub in winter with friends, a great job offer, requited love, unprovoked acts of kindness, a good book, *schadenfreude* when the bad guy gets his come-uppance, a risky gamble that pays off, a sense of humour, or the triumph of the underdog? We see confusing patterns emerge across Western culture. Conspicuous consumption, the desire for wealth and fame sit uneasily alongside the rise of therapy, 'emotional intelligence' and New Age twists on Eastern mysticism. In *Is America Breaking Apart?* John Hall and Charles Lindholm boiled down the American way to just four words: 'labour, accumulate, consume, display'. According to Freedman, the happy person is a 40-year-old woman who lives somewhere in Canada and works full time as an entertainer, earning Can.\$50,000 a year. Married for the first time, she loves her husband and leads a fairly active sex life, but she sometimes dreams of being Jacqueline Kennedy Onassis. She is a Unitarian, but is not especially religious and does not believe in ESP. She is an optimist by nature and believes that life has meaning and direction.

But is she really happy? Are we entitled even to ask the question? These days it seems enough for people to *say* they are happy for us to believe them (or at least, as I argue below, psychologists seem oddly satisfied with that as a definition). However much we may take people at face value, we can't help looking for evidence. As T. S. Eliot observed, 'we see them everywhere, those trying desperately for happiness: pitifully chasing clouds of butterflies, laughing too loud, drinking too much, buying too much, working too hard; hating themselves'. Whether we picture what researchers call 'peak experiences' or overall 'quality of life indicators', a simple look at how people seem to pursue or find happiness today indicates that the pursuit is as multifaceted and elusive as the concept itself.

In this chapter I briefly review the history of happiness, from philosophy and psychology, and reflect on how the term has only recently emerged as a product of social and political changes in the West. Travel across cultures or back through time and the question *Are you happy?* becomes less and less intelligible or relevant. Most places and epochs have stronger moral scripts than we do, and less room for self-contradiction. In tracing the history and shape of this question, I hope to show why the modern Western desire to be happy is a compelling yet paradoxical aspiration.

The Classical View

It has often been remarked that the history of philosophy is merely a series of footnotes to Plato, and the debates around happiness are no exception. The story starts with the Greek concept of *Eudaimonia* often (controversially) translated today as happiness. The word denotes an objective idea of a fulfilled, flourishing life worthy of praise. For Plato, happiness or virtue (which were the same thing in his world-view) resulted from psychic harmony between the three parts of our nature; reason, physical appetites and spiritual needs (for honour or success). This harmony was an abstract prescription linked with beauty and mathematical proportion and could only flourish in the right political setting, under a philosopher king.

Plato passed the baton to his student Aristotle, whose seminal book, *Nichomachean Ethics*, is the foundation stone of an incredibly influential tradition linking happiness with goodness.

> The Good of man is the active exercise of his soul's faculties in conformity with excellence or virtue ... Moreover this activity must occupy a complete lifetime; for one swallow does not make spring, nor does one fine day; and similarly one day or a brief period of happiness does not make a man supremely blessed and happy.

Aristotle's claim was that happiness is characterized by the attainment of virtue and excellence of character. Happiness is not a description of how one feels at any one time, rather it is an outcome of the noble conduct of one's life as a whole; the central thesis being that virtue brings its own reward. For Aristotle, using the doctrine of the Golden Mean, each virtue sits in a sort of Goldilocks happy medium between extremes. If we are courageous (neither cowardly nor rash), if we are modest (neither bashful nor shameless) and especially if we are magnanimous, more than humble and less than vain, happiness will be ours. Aristotle, more practical, less abstract than Plato, felt that a happy life required external goods to be complete, such as wealth and good luck.

This *Eudaimonistic* tradition is a common thread connecting the great philosophers of antiquity. Epicurus (contrary to modern associations of his name with self-indulgent pleasures) prescribed an even more self-denying ordinance than Aristotle. Pleasure was indeed the highest good, but since some pleasures depend on pain – in the way that pleasure in eating is connected to hunger and indigestion – we do well to stick to quiet undemanding pleasures. Epicurus (341–270 BC) himself lived on bread (though upgraded to cheese on feast days!). All we need do, he claimed, is to overcome (rather than indulge) our desire for pointless pleasures (food, drink, sex, etc.), as well as our fear of death, and by doing so achieve tranquillity (*ataraxia*).

The loftily indifferent Stoics such as Seneca (AD 1–50) and Epictetus (AD 50–130) similarly advocated giving up desiring the things we cannot have. Marcus Aurelius (AD 121–80), the great Stoic Roman emperor, meditated on the thought that we cannot rail against providence. We, the Stoics claimed, are part of a greater cosmos in which whatever happens is for the best, and so must take a dispassionate view of those things that are beyond our control and drop them as a distraction. Some modern commentators advise that we learn from these doctrines to help put things in perspective. Alain de Botton in the *Consolations of Philosophy* has been a prominent example of those offering comfort from ancient wisdom:

Terror. Recession. War. The modern world is fraught with insecurities. But there's little new about our woes: peace of mind has always been elusive. And, for thousands of years, the wise have had an answer. It's called Philosophy . . .

For all the common-sense value of suggesting we should 'be more stoical', work on things we can control and limit our desires to those that are in line with virtue rather than short term temptations, it is worth noting how far the terms of reference have slipped. The gulf between our moral and emotional sensitivity and those of 2,000 years ago is unbridgeable. Compare the modern father jagged by the pain of seeing his child bullied at school with the Stoic sage's response to the news that his son had been killed: 'What is that to me? I did not think that I had begat an immortal.' These tough-minded prescriptions go well beyond even Aristotle's recipe for the good life, which at least allowed that one needs external, worldly goods to be happy. By contrast the Epicurean or the Stoic could conceive of happiness on the rack if we follow their advice.

In general the point was that to call someone happy, in the *Eudaimonistic* tradition, was essentially a moral appraisal of their character and worthiness. This linking of virtue and the Good Life with happiness has been the corner stone of moral philosophy ever since and is still prevalent in current debates. Bertrand Russell described the *Nichomachean Ethics* as appealing to 'the respectable middle-aged, and has been used by them, especially since the seventeenth century, to repress the ardours and enthusiasms of the young. But to a man with any depth of feeling [like Russell himself, one assumes] it is likely to be repulsive.'[3] Kant exemplifies this continuing tradition with the dictum that morality is not properly the doctrine of how we make ourselves happy, but how we make ourselves worthy of happiness.

In the following centuries debates about happiness were largely the business of moral philosophers and the Church, and things got a lot bleaker! The development of Christianity raised the stakes for what constitutes a good life from a merely virtuous life to one that was sanctified by perfect goodness, by God. From this moment happiness was moved out of earthly reach, into the realms of eternity. Life was an unhappy struggle but, if we were worthy, would lead on to eternal happiness in heaven where the lion lies down with the lamb. This 'hair shirt' tradition is embodied in Martin Luther's formula for how to live, '*leiden, leiden, Kreuz, Kreuz*' (suffering, suffering, the Cross, the Cross), and angrily rejects *Glücklichkeit* (happiness) as a worthy aim. It finds its most highly evolved exemplars in the iconic images of St Jerome flagellating himself or Origen cutting off his own genitals. This forbidding religious version of the human condition was to dominate medieval culture for centuries.

The slow battle for retrieving the possibility of happiness on earth was begun by St Thomas Aquinas in the thirteenth century, and then taken up by the next generation of writers – Dante, for example – and those of the Renaissance. The shift was ultimately decisive despite strong resistance from the Church and other later critics of the secularization of happiness (such as Pascal in France in the seventeenth century). While the arguments between religious and ancient secular versions of happiness were still only offering different answers to the Socratic question *How ought I to live?*, the move away from religious constraints was a necessary platform for the emergence of a more subjective, psychological, some would say selfish, picture of happiness.

The Subjective Turn

Virtue as the reference point for discussions of happiness began to come under strain when political and social changes rendered the limitations of an account of happiness that had little room for personal pleasure impossible to ignore. The focus shifted to what moral philosophers call a 'prudential' view of the good – feeling good rather than being good. That inveterate iconoclast Bertrand Russell captures the spirit well.

> One should as a rule respect public opinion in so far as is necessary to avoid starvation and to keep out of prison, but anything that goes beyond this is voluntary submission to an unnecessary tyranny, and is likely to interfere with happiness in all kinds of ways.[4]

The historian Roy Porter recently outlined the rise of Enlightenment thinking, with its fondness for happiness and pleasure in a modern sense. He argues that while the Renaissance had still to some extent venerated the high ethics of the Ancients, the unruly politics and culture of the seventeenth and eighteenth centuries gave emancipatory rise to the feel-good factor. 'The auguries were auspicious: human nature was not flawed by the Fall; desire was desirable, society improvable, knowledge progressive and good would emerge from what Priestly dubbed man's "endless cravings".' Religious figures began to leaven their preachy injunctions with a nod to *vox populi*. 'Even the sober Joseph Butler, later a bishop, doubted we were justified in pursuing virtue, 'till we are convinced it will be for our happiness, or at least, not contrary to it.' Not much room for self-mutilation there! And philosophers went much further. Those of the Enlightenment and its aftermath, such as Hobbes, Locke, Hume, Bentham and Mill, and their Romantic confrères (such as Rousseau) fell over themselves to place happiness, desire, freedom, consciousness, self-expression and/or pleasure at the heart of the modern moral economy.

Thus heartened, Albion's polite and commercial people seized their chance to express themselves, to escape the iron cage of Calvinism, custom and kinship – even to indulge their whims. Acquisitiveness, pleasure-seeking, emotional and erotic self-discovery, social climbing and the joys of fashion slipped the moral and religious straightjackets of guilt, sin and retribution.[5]

This new form of self-expression redefined happiness once and for all. In earlier times, one might say, the concept simply did not exist. This is a large claim. It's difficult to accept that people living centuries ago had no sense, that we Moderns would recognize, of whether they were happy. Surely we're all basically the same and always have been? Intuitively it is almost impossible to imagine anything else. We can't but see our ancestors through a contemporary lens when our versions of Ben Hur, Cleopatra and Spartacus have all the emotional and individualistic psychology of Charlton Heston, Elizabeth Taylor and Kirk Douglas. Yet despite this difficulty, historians and social scientists have attempted to offer glimpses of historical periods in their own terms by studying the language of the time. If you see emotions primarily as defined through their social functions rather than simple physical states (as researchers increasingly are arguing we should[6]), then when these social functions change, so should the way we describe emotions. Nobody, they claim, would today experience *accidie*: an extinct emotion meaning, roughly, the sin of sloth or a disgust in one's failure to take pleasure from one's religious duty. We don't talk much of melancholy any more, though we do obsess today with forms of clinical depression.

The social psychologist Derek Edwards draws on the *Oxford English Dictionary* to trace the changing definition of the term *emotion* itself. This clearly reveals a shift in its usage from the realm of action to the realm of feeling:

1. A moving out, migration, transference from one place to another. Obs. 1695 Woodward *Nat. Hist. Earth* i. (1723) 45 Some accidental Emotion . . . of the Center of Gravity.

2. A moving, stirring, agitation, perturbation (in physical sense). Obs. 1708 O. Bridgman in *Phil Trans.* xxvi. 138 Thunder . . . caused so great an Emotion in the Air.

3. transf. A political or social agitation; a tumult, popular disturbance. Obs. 1579 Fenton Guicciard. ii, There were . . . great stirres and emocions in Lombardye

4. a. fig. Any agitation or disturbance of mind feeling, passion; any vehement or excited mental state. 1762 Kames *Elem. Crit.* ii. x2. (1833) 37 The joy of gratification is properly called an emotion.

The current 'psychological' meaning is given as originating in the late eighteenth century, as follows:

Psychology. A mental 'feeling' or 'affection' (e.g. of pleasure or pain, desire or aversion, surprise, hope or fear, etc.), as distinguished from cognitive or volitional states of consciousness. Also abstr. 'feeling' as distinguished from the other classes of mental phenomena.[7]

With the rise of emotions as inner drivers of human behaviour, coinciding with the rise of the new discipline of psychology, came a turning-point in history of extraordinary significance. The pursuit of happiness, moving from its early connotation of good fortune and good character addressing the

Socratic question *How ought I to live?*, came to require that we answer a brand new question, namely *What do I really want?* This trend, away from the moral, toward individual needs has gathered uneven pace ever since, opening up a clear contrast between happiness in the *Eudaimonistic* tradition and what people search for now. The story has not been without its reverses. Any victim of religious zealotry, Victorian prudery or the moral majoritarianism of the 1950s will know the cost of pushing liberation too far or too fast. Yet, despite these counters, the general trend has been clear, and has accelerated over the last half-century. If the God's-eye view has dropped out of the sky and churches are no longer the tallest buildings, it is no surprise that we just see things differently. Only when it began to be possible to see happiness as dependent on a more subjective, personal ideal did the modern term become intelligible.

If the past is another country when it comes to the modern pursuit of happiness, some would say this is equally true of other countries and cultures. V. S. Naipaul said he was attracted to the West by

> the beauty of the idea of the pursuit of happiness . . . This idea . . . is at the heart of the attractiveness of the civilization to so many outside it or on its periphery . . . It implies a certain kind of society, a certain kind of awakened spirit. I don't imagine my father's Hindu parents would have been able to understand the idea. So much is contained in it: the idea of the individual, responsibility, choice, the life of the intellect, the idea of vocation and perfectibility and achievement. It is an immense human idea. It cannot be reduced to a fixed system. It cannot generate fanaticism. But it is known to exist, and because of that, other more rigid systems in the end blow away.

Many would claim that the rampant individualism that makes happiness intelligible to us makes it as obscure to other cultures as it is to other periods in our history. Our preoccupation can look like a parochial Western obsession predicated on a picture of the self floating free from its social and cultural context. The anthropologist Clifford Geertz once remarked that:

> the Western conception of the person as a bounded, unique, more or less integrated motivational and cognitive universe, a dynamic center of awareness, emotion, judgment, and action organized into a distinctive whole and set contrastively both against other such wholes and against a social and natural background is, however incorrigible it may seem to us, a rather peculiar idea within the context of the world's cultures.[8]

There are many problematic implications of the claim that happiness is a culturally bounded concept. At the very least the pervasiveness of Western culture, and our Macdonaldized consumer society, corrupts the notion of self-contained cultures necessary to supporting the thesis. For my purposes it is enough to say that the history of happiness shows that today's use of the term is a recent development and that it cannot be applied to other periods in history. Whether the same could be said of the use of happiness as a concept across cultures is, on my view, an open question.

The Politics of Happiness

The shift from a moral to a more psychological view coincided with the rise of happiness as a political concept in the late eighteenth century. Thomas Jefferson famously enshrined the concept in the American Constitution:

> We hold these truths to be self-evident, that all men are created equal, that they are endowed by their Creator with certain unalienable rights, that among these are life, liberty and the pursuit of happiness.

The sentiment was echoed in the *French Declaration of Human Rights* (1789), whose first line reads 'The goal of society is common happiness.' The new politics after the Enlightenment was fixated on understanding how to control and promote happiness through political and cultural institutions. The spirit of the times was captured by the Jacobin leader Armand St Just: 'happiness' – *le bonheur* – 'is a new idea in Europe'.

The central role of happiness in political analysis was furthered in the development of Utilitarianism. Bentham's famous dictum that 'The greatest happiness of the greatest number is the foundation of morals and legislation' set the problem up as a scientific challenge to maximize pleasure and minimize pain. While the Utilitarians had the advantage of a nice, clean and coherent theory, they had great difficulty applying it in practice. Not only did the theory break free of any moral bearings (if it feels good, do it), it led to paradoxical attempts to compare large amounts of pleasure for small numbers of people with its converse. If there was no provision for different *qualities* of pleasure, then Bentham had to conclude that 'quantity of pleasure being equal, pushpin is as good as poetry'. Mill later struggled with this rampant egalitarianism and decided that one had to distinguish between higher and lower orders of pleasure: 'it is better to be a human being dissatisfied than a pig satisfied; better to be Socrates dissatisfied than a fool satisfied', and if the fool or the pig disagree 'it is because they only know their own side of the question. The other party to the comparison knows both sides.'[9] Either way, egalitarian or elitist, this 'felicific calculus' could never quantify happiness in any way that could drive a political and legal system.

Happiness has not fared well as a political concept despite the optimism of the Enlightenment. At the heart of the problem is the question *What kind of happiness does this unalienable right entitle us to pursue?* Whether the founding fathers were thinking of the modern pursuit of well-feeling and self-expression or the ancient *Eudaimonistic* path to virtue is unclear. What is clear is that it is the former interpretation that dominates Western society today, as reflected in the growth of therapy, self-help and other routes to self-actualization, while the older, more obsolete question still leaves us uneasy.

The reason that the concept of happiness makes bad politics is that since it is so hard to define it can easily be invoked to justify all forms of action. One of Solzhenitsyn's characters in *Cancer Ward* makes the point:

> Happiness is a mirage . . . [f]or that happiness I burned books that contained truth. This applies even more to the so-called 'happiness of future generations.' Who can foresee it? Who has talked with these future generations, who knows what other idols they will yet bow down to? Ideas of happiness have changed too much down the centuries to foresee how to prepare for it in advance. When we have white loaves to trample under our heels and we're choking on milk, it won't make us happy at all. But if we shared our meager portion, we could be happy right now! If we think only of 'happiness' and 'growth', we shall fill up the earth senselessly and create a frightening society.[10]

Happiness fails as a political concept because it can be turned to any purpose, given the term's ambivalent connotations. Either virtue is part of its definition and so it becomes a set of moral or societal injunctions, or it is replaced by the feel-good factor that opens up the possibility that anything goes. At the political level the concept is either anodyne or dangerous. The pursuit of happiness can only make any sense when you scale down from the political sphere to the level of individual psychology.

The False Hope of Psychology

By the beginning of the twentieth century the terms of reference for debates on happiness had shifted decisively. In the face of a preoccupation with subjective feelings of satisfaction, moral philosophy for the most part dropped out of the reckoning. The analysis of happiness became an intellectual backwater in philosophy, while the new discipline of psychology ushered in a surge of empirical research on the topic.

The vast growth of research on happiness during this century was almost entirely in the social sciences, with a sharp increase in the last three decades. The world database of happiness (there is indeed such a thing) has identified 16 scholarly articles published before 1900, 22 between 1900 and 1930, 99 between then and 1960 and a partial listing of nearly 3,000 papers since 1960 in the social sciences alone. (This does not include the huge rise of pop psychology literature devoted to this theme.) One might paraphrase Larkin and say that happiness was invented in 1963.

Pop psychology books on the secrets of a happy life by therapeutic gurus fill our bookshops, and more bookshelves at home than their possessors are usually willing to admit. Like diet books, the appetite for them seems to be limitless. The sheer tonnage of titles should give the reader pause, since, if the prescriptions worked, no person would really need more than one. Of course it is not that simple – these books probably all say something of relevance and can give anybody food for thought, while never being life transforming (despite their over-excited blurbs). Broadly, they offer commonsensical prescriptions for this intractable and pervasive theme – predictable advice in the tradition of self-help and positive thinking. But the problem with common sense is that it ends up pointing us in several directions at once. Do we believe that absence makes the heart grow fonder? Or that out of sight is out of mind? Do more hands make light work, or do they spoil the broth when attached to too many cooks? Look before you leap, but don't forget that he who hesitates is lost . . . And so on.

So it is with the nostrums from the happiness merchants. A favourite quote of the gurus is Nathaniel Hawthorne's 'Happiness is as a butterfly, which, when pursued, is always just beyond our grasp, but which, if you will sit down quietly, may alight upon you.' By contrast, in *Psycho-Cybernetics*

2000, Bobbe L. Sommer exhorts you to 'recognize that you'll find the path to your goal much smoother if you consciously *choose* happiness.' He adds 'there is only one right time to make your move to happiness: *now*. You can make happiness a habit in the same way you make any other attitudes and behavior a habit – through conscious, repeated practice until it has become a subconscious act.' Chase that butterfly!

Allain (pseudonym of the French philosopher Emile Chartier) offers practical advice on how to '*will* one's happiness and create it'. *The Little Book of Happiness* advises that we 'do good . . . earn praise . . . earn thanks (but take great care not to demand them)', while *The 9 Steps to Lifelong Happiness* recommends 'knowing your internal self and responding to your real needs, rather than the demands of others'. Be brave enough to change, and take the road less travelled, but be content with your lot and realize that *Men are from Mars and Women are from Venus*. Put yourself first and put yourself last. These books are numerous, self-contradictory and often have short shelf lives.

Professional psychology on this topic doesn't fare much better. In fact, much psychological research on happiness, based on self-reports and analysed by self-styled 'eudologists', is embarrassingly bad and almost indistinguishable from the pop version. The social psychologist Michael Argyle has drawn together conclusions from a large review of this research, concluding:

> Short term increases in positive mood can be induced by thinking about recent pleasant events, watching funny films or TV, listening to cheerful music, and to some extent by reciting positive self statements, by smiles, jokes, small presents and hypnosis. The effects tend to be rather brief, but these activities can be engaged in regularly. The only drug which seems to be successful is alcohol, but in doses which are not too large.[11]

As one reviewer comments, 'it must give some readers pause that after the study and collation of more than three hundred studies the author advises us to "watch funny films or TV"'.[12]

One problem with the methodology of self-reports (where you take people's answers to the question *Are you happy?* at face value) is that it becomes impossible to evaluate claims. It becomes impossible to say – She claims to be happy but is she really? Some might ask – What is wrong with that? In the current *zeitgeist* the happiness of well-feeling means that we can declare ourselves happy and that is all the proof we need. Yet we also know that if we go too far down this route we move towards a Brave New Prozac Nation. We know that there is something basically unsatisfying about having things too easily within our grasp. Like filling up on fries or crisps, easy pleasure is not always nourishing. The sense of challenge was once clear, we had morals and virtues (whether *Eudaimonistic* or religious) that provided the hurdle we needed to overcome. Now we can do what we like without having to account for it, and while the freedom is intoxicating, it is not much fun playing tennis with the net down.

As a result of too much psychology we have rediscovered a taste for morality. Our freedom has aroused a desire for bigger ideas or better clubs to belong to. We have been examining our navels ever since they were uncovered, and have been frankly disappointed by what we have found. Unfortunately, we cannot return to the big themes of old that we so successfully discredited. Churches now are just so much architecture. We have had to invent alternatives utopias, return to nature or mysticism, worship celebrities, fashion cultures and counter-cultures in what we call our New Age. Alongside the cult of the individual has arisen cult of the cult.

Happiness today is elusive because it poses a dilemma. We are compelled by our time to move from the standardization of our moral careers to the customization of our desires. This lurch towards the freedom to shape our destiny has been decisive and seems to be accelerating. We have choices now but do not know what lights by which to be guided in making them. We are baffled. Freedom alone is not enough; yet ancient sources of guidance look cramped and outdated in their calls to sources of moral authority (whether God or God substitutes) that are no longer authoritative, so we must turn to something else.

Feeling Free versus Feeling Justified

So our pursuit of happiness requires us to answer the question *What do I really want?* in the light of its antique counterpart, *How ought I to live?* The first question I see as an expression of the need to feel free, while the second represents the need to feel justified. The fact that we are riven by conflict, and that competing needs lie at the heart of the human condition, is a commonplace when one looks at theories from across the social sciences. Freud famously pitted the unruly *id* (a 'seething cauldron of excitement'), exclusively devoted to answering the question *What do I really want?*, against the *super-ego*'s moral injunctions on how we ought to live.

Similar themes abound in much academic work on self and identity. Taking his cue from Freud, the literary theorist Lionel Trilling contrasted *sincerity* (the civilized loyalty of Hamlet's friend Horatio) against *authenticity* (the atavistic desire of Conrad's Mr Kurtz). In existential philosophy, Jean-Paul Sartre's concept of 'bad faith' is based on the central tension between our 'in itself' or *facticity* made up of our 'situation', our connections to others, etc., and the 'for itself', the *transcendence* that enables us to step outside of our habits and seize on possibilities. And on it goes . . . In sociology there is Weber's distinction between *self-fashioning* and *self-discipline*. In psychology various academics contrast *personal* with *social identity*. In management, consultants work up Abraham Maslow's hierarchy of needs to distinguish between the *inner-directed* people motivated by self-actualization and the *outer-directed* people motivated by social esteem and status. Anthropologists like Richard Shweder identify *autonomy* and *community* (along with *purification*) as the core moral spheres of any society.

These variations on a theme are complex, distinctive theories drawing on surprisingly discrete intellectual traditions, literatures and canons despite their obvious points of overlap. They interest me insofar as they bear on a widespread recognition that human beings are deeply self-contradictory in their needs; more specifically that these contradictions come up around the contemporary ideal of the *need to feel free* and a modern expression of the ancient *need to feel justified*. These requirements are obviously in tension with each other. The need for freedom requires a developed sense of agency, authorship, being in control of events rather than controlled by them, and is connected to privatized feelings of uniqueness. The need to feel justified today is about overcoming meaninglessness (a new malaise) and a desire for belonging and applause. It has a moral dimension (unlike freedom) and requires submission to a fitting audience – to bow to our judges and give up our freedom. In particular, this need for justification can no longer be met by gods and traditions as it was for centuries, and still is in some cultures. In modern Western society it can only be sought from other people. Morality has become privatized.

I choose these terms as those least likely to lead to mistaken connotations, but in fact they are merely place-holders for a whole set of behaviours that reflect our ambivalence towards people, language and rules. *Freedom* represents the need to turn away from people, escape from language and break rules. *Justification* represents the need to bow to norms and seek applause. This is what I mean by the Happiness Paradox: *a modern sensibility both wants to break free and wants to belong.*

More evidence for this claim comes from those who analyse sadness and self-destruction. In *Malignant Sadness*, a book on clinical depression, Lewis Wolpert identifies two key correlates with depression: feeling trapped and feeling humiliated. The first is the frustration of our desire for freedom: the second is the frustration of our desire to feel justified. Relatedly, Emile Durkheim identified two prominent forms of suicide; the first, *egoistic suicide*, is where people are so privatized that they totally fail to integrate with others; the second, *altruistic suicide*, is where people die for a cause – i.e., they subjugate themselves totally in some form of social structure. These, respectively, are the limit points of the desire for freedom and the desire for justification.

As I argue later in this book, when people complain about their work or their relationships (the two key ingredients of a happy life, according to Freud), the trouble comes down to one of two things. Either they lack freedom, i.e., they feel trapped or bored; or they lack justification, and so feel humiliated, exploited or rejected. And as they try to rectify the lack, they run further risks. Those who pursue justification too earnestly start to look craven or needy. Those who pursue freedom too exclusively look selfish, childish or mad. The painful fact is that the desire for freedom directly contradicts the desire for justification. The pursuit of happiness is an expression of the desire to solve the freedom versus justification dilemma: related tensions – short term versus long term, anxiety versus boredom, progress versus tradition – pervade our daily thought and action. Going back to the *Nichomachean Ethics* one could ask if there is a Golden Mean between freedom and justification to help us attain the virtue of happiness. In this book I argue that the liberating, but heartbreaking, answer is *No*. We gave up on that kind of authority long ago.

It has probably always been characteristic of the human condition that too little and too much are equally destructive, as Aristotle claimed. Only now, with no objective moral compass to direct us, there is no script to tell us how to avoid each danger. To make this more concrete, imagine you are working as an assistant in a shop and the owner leaves for the afternoon expecting you to wax the floor. How do you know the appropriate amount of waxing to do? If you don't wax at all you are cheating the owner; if you wax a little and quickly tire, you are lazy or selfish; if you wax too much you are craven, over-eager to impress; and if you wax all afternoon you're simply mad. We are almost always plagued with a sense of doing too much or too little. Unfortunately (and fortunately), there is no fact of the matter; it is a matter of opinion. Relativists would claim that this means 'anything goes': we can do what we like as long as it feels good. On the contrary, without a god's-eye view to guide our choices, we are more dependent than ever on mere opinion (from people who count).

Not trying hard enough, or trying too hard. These two fears loom large in our culture and can make the pursuit of freedom or justification simply too risky. We call the first commitment phobia, and Erica Jong called the second *Fear of Flying*. Freedom and justification in a flattering light are to do with bold self-reliance and honourable selflessness respectively. In a less-flattering light they make us look either selfish or craven. Where once we might have hoped for a fruitful synthesis, we are now left with an arid paradox.

There is something in W. B. Yeats's poem 'Vacillation' that captures a momentary fusion of these needs:

My 50th year had come and gone,
I sat, a solitary man
in a crowded London shop,
an open book, an empty cup
on the marble table top.

While on the shop and street I gazed
my body of a sudden blazed!
And twenty minutes more or less
it seemed so great my happiness
that I was blesséd – and could bless.[13]

But of course, according to common sense, momentary happiness is not the same as happiness on the whole, over time. Commentators tend to focus on one or the other, short versus long term, by contrasting 'peak experiences' with 'life satisfaction indicators'. Typically, *well-feeling* is framed as happiness in the short term, while the traditional ethical view is about the longer term (one sparrow does not make a spring, etc.). But this is a false dichotomy. By separating the short term from the long term, researchers conveniently overlook the fact that, in everyday usage, *happy* seems to describe each version equally well. My claim is that necessary to either short-term blazing or long-term contentment is a feeling that we are *truly* justified – meaning that we feel *both* free and justified. But this is not a happy medium, it is an unstable state. These needs both feed off and oppose each other. Wanting to be justified is all about turning towards others, and wanting to be free is about turning away.

This is why there are no easy synonyms for *happiness*. Embedded in the concept lies the synthesis of two antithetical needs. Looked at in this way we can see why the alternative terms cited as this chapter's epigraph are neither irrelevant to, nor quite right for, a description of happiness. At first sight it may appear that they are each placed at different points on a continuum, with freedom on one side and justification on the other. Bliss, ecstasy, elation might seem to be more about freedom, while contentment, peace of mind and self-esteem lean towards justification. But it is not that simple. Freedom and justification are complex and deeply interrelated needs. They are not contrasting poles at each end of a straight line. Rather, they form a vicious, or virtuous, circle, with each being central to the experience of the other.

On my account, the need to feel free is a complex of related forms (eroticism, artistic expression, voyages of discovery), and similarly the need to feel justified has as multifaceted and subtle a range (from longing for love to needing to feel proud). They are often hard to distinguish, and at heart they lead into each other. We need to feel free to feel truly justified, and we need to feel justified to feel truly free. My chapters Two and Three deliberately force these concepts apart in order to discuss them more deeply. I start with our urge to be free. I explore the depth of our need for it, and argue for its being a necessary, if self-refuting, condition for human happiness.

CHAPTER TWO

Feeling Free

The challenge of modern freedom, or the combination of isolation and freedom which confronts you, is to make yourself up. The danger is that you may emerge from the process as a not-entirely-human creature.

Saul Bellow, *Ravelstein*[1]

Why do people bankrupt themselves on a roll of the dice? Why do they jump off bridges attached to a piece of elastic? Why does a poet spend days searching for the perfect phrase, or people climb mountains because 'they're there'? Why does an American president risk his place in history for a sexual encounter? Why do people get tattoo'd, or say things just to shock? In answering these questions people often reach for words like adventure, self-expression, fantasy, ambition. These words all bear on what I mean by the need for freedom. I am not attempting to engage directly with philosophical and sociological debates about negative versus positive liberty, free will versus determinism, or the social contract. My concern is to describe something of the subtlety and compelling nature of the psychological need to *feel* free (even if we never are in some abstract sense) – what Chomsky calls 'the essential and defining property of man'.

The traditional preoccupation with happiness, as described in chapter One, was once firmly rooted in the pursuit of virtue. Today, by contrast, we take the principles of self-determination and autonomy for granted, in Western society at least, as necessary for a happy life. We need to feel we are in control of events rather than controlled by them, and that we are in some way authors of our own destiny; the ultimate consolation for disappointment is that at least, like Frank Sinatra, 'I did it my way'. At the same time, the expression of this need is derided by many, as shallow, narcissistic and selfish. The trashy excesses of consumer culture, the loss of enduring values and self-respect and the belief that 'there is no such thing as society', are bemoaned as leading to threadbare, disconnected and unhappy lives. While I will address these fears further, my aim in this chapter is to set out why this need to feel free is so overpowering, and that whatever dangers come with it we must embrace and understand it if we want to understand happiness.

Moreover, this is a complex need that manifests itself in quite distinct ways. If I were writing 50 years ago it would have been natural to take my cue from Freud and reduce this need to unconscious drives for sex and aggression. While this characterization may capture some of the subversive and unruly elements of the need for freedom, we need to balance those with some of its more inspiring features. In fact, freedom in the sense I am using it is a complex and textured array of overlapping notions that includes discovery, authenticity, independence, artistic creation, escape, bliss, uniqueness, irony, will, power, self-indulgence, fantasy, transgression, perversion, comedy, desire, genius, the call of the wild and the 'search for strange'.

The cultural celebrations of this urge as the source of heroism and individual self-fulfilment fill our books and films. Maya Angelou's *I Know Why the Caged Bird Sings*, and Rita in the film *Educating Rita* looking for a 'better song to sing', capture the familiar idea of freedom as about finding one's authentic voice. By the same token, wanting to be free, as I argue later, is a desire to escape from the language of others, from words that turn us into stereotypes and generalizations. Freedom celebrates the particular against the general, the fresh metaphor against the cliché.

The Invention of Freedom

The need to feel free is a taste for the unruly. A desire not to compromise, not to bend to other's whims and norms. Like our concept of happiness, its current expression has a relatively recent and local history.[2] Until the development of an individualistic or romantic conception of the self, there was little alternative to the social norms that defined people's station and role in life in relation to God or monarchy or codes or honour. Rousseau shattered this picture with the famous insight that 'man is born free, and everywhere he is in chains'. He articulated and crystallized these unruly currents for generations to come:

> Nature commands every animal and the beast obeys. Man feels the same impetus, but he realizes he is free to acquiesce or resist; and it is above all in the consciousness of his freedom that the spirituality of his soul is shown.[3]

Rousseau railed against contemporary civilization and mores, with a call to release our true natures from the oppression of social convention. The impact of this picture of a natural self residing beneath the artificial layers of social crust and waiting to break free had a revolutionary effect in its day. In a similar vein, Schelling announced that 'the beginning and end of all Philosophy is – Freedom' and that 'the time has come to proclaim to a nobler humanity the freedom of the spirit, and no longer to have patience with men's tearful regrets for their lost chains'.[4]

The twentieth century bore witness to the consequences of increasing freedom, and its pursuit was never more celebrated or more vilified. In posing the question *What do I really want?* the need for freedom can be an inspiring call to arms, or a recipe for self-annihilation. The clichés tell the story: 'Seize the day' or 'Take the road less travelled' vie with 'An evil man is a child grown strong' and 'There is no such thing as society' for attempts to characterize the urge to be free. In *Drift and Mastery* Walter Lippman commented,

> what nonsense it is then to talk of liberty as if it were a happy go lucky breaking of chains . . . Liberty is a searching challenge, for it takes away the guardianship of the master and the comfort of the priest. The iconoclasts didn't free us. They threw us into the water and now we have to swim.[5]

The philosopher Charles Taylor usefully contrasts the pro-freedom 'boosters', who relish escape, self-expression and the permissive society, with modernity's 'knockers', who believe that modern individualism is taking us to hell in a handcart. To the latter, too much freedom is a bad thing. Words of warning urging the stern need for constraints to leash the beast come from academics, religious leaders, journalists and all manner of cultural commentators invoking higher lights by which we should be guided. They berate the feckless 'youth of today', who have no respect for their elders and betters, and who surf on a rising tide of sex and violence. Frequently, the exuberant boosters are represented by popular culture and contrast with the furrow-browed knockers of high culture. Mass media, the consumer society, management gurus, therapists and Hollywood provide relentless paeans to freedom and self-expression, while the high priests of high culture typically wring their hands (while dreaming of wringing necks!).

A typical example comes from Robert Bellah's co-study of American culture, *Habits of the Heart*, a pained critique of the American Dream in a tradition that leads back to Tocqueville: 'Clearly the meaning of one's life for most Americans is to become one's own person, almost to give birth to oneself.' 'Much of this process', he says, 'is negative. It involves breaking free from family, community and inherited ideas.'

> Even those trapped in the language of the isolated self ('in the end you're really alone') are troubled by the nihilism they sense there and eager to find a way of overcoming the emptiness of purely arbitrary 'values'.

Bellah proposes that Western (especially American) culture is on the brink of disaster. His book as a whole is a response to the question *How can we avoid the slide into the abyss?*[6] People, he argues, feel all at sea and badly need an anchor.

Bellah's prescriptions echo the ranks of great and good all offering their brand of moral fibre as improving grist to our dark satanic mills. In a passage from a letter to his wife, Freud reveals this barely concealed contempt: 'it is neither pleasant nor edifying to watch the masses amuse themselves . . . the mob gives vent to its appetites and we (the refined) deprive ourselves . . . we save ourselves for something, not knowing what . . . to maintain our integrity'.[7] All the more striking to hear it from the inventor of the pleasure principle!

One can understand why the knockers berate the culture of decline. The fabric of society is undeniably threadbare in places: crime levels, divorce rates, lifestyle infomercials (one of which I saw recently advertised a product called 'exercise in a bottle'), the 'dumbing down' of news and education are oft-cited indicators that we are a long way down the 'slippery slope' to the loss of enduring values that make life worth living.

Yet Rousseau would have been stunned by the high-minded vilification that pours from the pens of the great and the good. He confronts those who resist the need to be free, 'who boast incessantly of the peace and repose they enjoy in their chains', by saying

> When I see the others sacrifice pleasures, repose, wealth, power, and life itself for the preservation of this sole good which is so disdained by those who have lost it . . . I feel that it does not behove slaves to reason about freedom.

In contemporary society Rousseau is on the side of the boosters, and popular culture (from *The Great Escape* to *Cry Freedom*) celebrates his insight.

A relatively rare, serious-minded defence of freedom comes from the philosopher Charles Taylor, who argues, contrary to the knockers, that its pursuit is underpinned by 'a deeper moral vision'. His is a view of freedom as something ennobling and inspiring. He counsels against criticizing modernity by focusing on the worst of it, namely 'pride, self-satisfaction [and] liberation from demanding standards' and other such 'trivial and self-indulgent forms'.[8] Taylor supports neither the uncritical boosters nor the pessimistic knockers – his project is to recover the ideal of authenticity as a 'moral source'.

The problem the knockers have with freedom is its corrosive, amoral quality, and Taylor's response is in effect to say something like – Well, if you look at its most noble expression (and overlook its more trivial and self indulgent forms), it proves more moral and less corrosive than it may seem at first. He wants to dignify it as 'an orientation towards the good'; he wants us to be free to pursue 'the sacred' 'the important questions'.[9] But there is something wrong with Taylor's noble-minded attempt to dignify freedom as a moral source (dignity belongs under justification in my book). In raising the moral status of the need for freedom, Taylor has lost the spontaneous, unruly and subversive quality that makes it so compelling. In the process he has tamed freedom in order to admire it, and by doing so has turned it into something else. Taylor's civilized freedom is ultimately complicit in the moral majoritarian view by claiming something deep and reassuringly humourless about the freedom urge – it is a 'moral source' – and that is why we should give it a better press.

We need to celebrate freedom without denying its corrosive qualities; even to admire those very qualities. It is a central driver of much that is great in modern civilization, and the knockers make themselves irrelevant for failing to attempt a serious understanding of such a fundamental force. The urge to be free is neither moral nor immoral; it does not lie on that axis.

If Taylor flinches from embracing the freedom he claims to admire, the same case can be made against Rousseau, whose argument from nature depends on his intuitively optimistic view of people. His radicalism is offset by a benign conception of how we look deep down.

> Take from our hearts this love of what is noble and you rob us of the joy of life. The mean-spirited man in whom these delicious feelings have been stifled among vile passions, who by thinking of no-one but himself comes at last to love no-one but himself, this man feels no raptures, his cold heart no longer throbs with joy, and his eyes no longer fill with the sweet tears of sympathy, he delights in nothing; the wretch has neither life nor feeling, he is already dead.[10]

By discreetly moving the moral over into the natural, Rousseau embeds the highest ideals of society into our very nature – a truly free, unsocialized nature would look at the world through eyes that fill 'with sweet tears of sympathy'. But this optimistic thesis is not persuasive. In a discussion of cruelty, Richard Rorty makes a compelling case that the unruly nature of our yearning for freedom, our 'intelligence, judgment, curiosity, imagination, a taste for beauty have no more connection with some central region of the self – a "natural" self which prefers kindness to torture, or torture to kindness – than do muscular limbs or sensitive genitals.'[11] Unfortunately for Rousseau and Taylor, the urge to be free is quite independent of the need to be good. If we let go of social structure we might not be noble-hearted heroes, but we could lose ourselves in a morass of atavistic desires – in Conrad's heart of darkness.

Despite this undue optimism, Rousseau provided the tools with which others could sculpt a far less-constrained search for the inner self, and underpinned a major shift in our culture and identity. If freedom's contemporary defender, Charles Taylor, is too high-minded to give the urge full credit, we need only go back to the nineteenth century to hear those who truly celebrate it without qualm or qualification.

The Call of the Wild

Henry David Thoreau built a small cabin on the property called Walden Pond that belonged to his friend and mentor Ralph Waldo Emerson. He moved in on 4 July 1845, and his book *Walden; or Life in the Woods* describes his life during the two years he lived there. A devout believer in simplicity, he warned: 'Beware of all enterprises that require new clothes, and not rather a new wearer of clothes.' He thrived on the solitary life, and commented that 'what men call social virtue, good fellowship, is commonly but the virtue of pigs in a litter, which lie close together to keep each other warm.' Famously he declared that 'the mass of men lead lives of quiet desperation. What is called resignation is confirmed desperation.' His defence of one version of freedom is completely uncompromising.

> I went to the woods because I wished to live deliberately, to front only the essential facts of life, and see if I could not learn what it had to teach, and not, when I came to die, discover that I had not lived . . . I wanted to live deep and suck out all of the marrow of life, to live so sturdily and Spartanlike as to put to rout all that was not life, to cut a broad swath and shave close, to drive life into a corner, and reduce it to its lowest terms.[12]

One of the enduring representations of the need for freedom is the voyage of discovery or the call of the wild. This explorer spirit can take the form of muscular can-do, overcoming obstacles to open up new vistas. By the same token it can describe the inward voyage to discover our true selves. The metaphor of the American journey, as in Kerouac's *On the Road* or taking 'the road less travelled', is a recurrent theme in pop psychology and goes back to Walt Whitman:

> Afoot and light-hearted I take to the open road,
> Healthy, free, the world before me
> The long brown path before, leading wherever I choose . . .[13]

One of the iconic documents of this pilgrim conception of freedom comes in Emerson's famous essay, 'Self-Reliance'. Emerson venerated the child's insouciance, 'the non-chalance of boys who are sure of a dinner', as unconcerned about the future and past and other people. They run naked and free:

> What pretty oracles nature yields us on this text in the face and behavior of children, babes and even brutes! . . . Their mind

being whole, *their eye is as yet unconquered*, and when we look in their faces we are disconcerted. (emphasis added)

In this vein he sets up an argument that ends in the celebration of authenticity, and in many ways lays the foundation for the therapeutic rhetoric of the 'child within' and the search for basic inner truths that are so fundamental to the modern American self concept. 'What I must do is all that concerns me, not what the people think.'[14] Break away from the erosion of our 'self trust', he urges, from consistency, 'the hobgoblin of little minds', and from conformity, which 'loses your time and blurs the impression of your character'. Emerson's strenuous and strident prose vividly rages against imitation, compromise and envy, seeing them as the source of unnatural living, cowardice and bad faith. 'Nothing can bring you peace but yourself. Nothing can bring you peace but the triumph of principles.'

This search for discovery and authenticity has had an impressive effect on American culture, both in the power of the 'can do' spirit and in the pursuit of self-actualization that is so redolent of California. That this vision is peculiarly American was reaffirmed by Walter Lippman:

> . . . the American dream, which may be summed up, I think, in the statement that the undisciplined man is the salt of the earth. So when the trusts appeared, when the free land was gone, America had been congested into a nation, the only philosophy with any weight of tradition behind it was a belief in the virtues of the spontaneous, enterprising, untrained and unsocialised man.[15]

This pursuit of self-expression and discovery is a powerful organizing principle for American society today, and thanks to Hollywood is one of its most powerful exports. The sociologist Philip Rieff calls it 'the rise of psychological man' (in his book *The Triumph of the Therapeutic*). This form of the search for freedom is about overcoming artificial obstacles (whether external or internal) that keep us from 'the truth' – for many in the West, the heart of what people love and loathe about contemporary American culture.

Freedom as Self-Creation

While the pilgrim spirit of adventure and discovery described above is a potent form of the urge to be free, it can be contrasted with the artist's urge for freedom as self-creation. Yeats once commented that all happiness 'depends on the energy to assume the mask of some other self; that all joyous or creative life is a rebirth as something not oneself, something which has no memory and is created in a moment and perpetually renewed.'

Whether in poetry's move from Romanticism to Modernism or, after the development of photography, the shift in the visual arts from representation to Expressionism and abstraction, it is the case that beauty, transgression and disruption have overtaken verisimilitude as the dominant aims of today's artist. The development into maturity of the European novel, one of the chief achievements of nineteenth-century culture, is described by Milan Kundera as the 'art inspired by God's laughter', capturing the essence of the novel as sublime yet subversive.

The sustained creativity of an artistic soul is more often fantasized than experienced. As Emerson observed, when we watch a young child playing alone we see spontaneous creativity and self-expression in a purer form than is permitted in our own lives. This imaginative engagement with the world, this 'unconquered eye', is something we fear is lost through the compromises of ageing. In our daydreams we hope that having put away childish things we might at least be able, like Einstein, to retain the capacity for child-like wonder and picture the world as a canvas on which to paint 'the mask of some other self'. These imaginary other lives are free of the constraints and obligations that pin us down, and in a Yeatsian 'rebirth' let us revel in counter-factual greatness. But the moment passes and we soon know, as Oscar Wilde did, that while we are all lying in the gutter *only some of us* are looking at the stars.

One archetypal star-gazer was Vladimir Nabokov, whose quest for aesthetic bliss over mere worldly concerns (and the 'topical trash' of those who write about them) is expressed well in his *Lectures on Literature,* where he consistently admires style over substance. Nabokov says a good reader will read with the spine not the brain. The rationalizations of the brain are strictly for those who are 'immune to the aesthetic vibrancy of authentic literature, for those who do not experience the tell-tale tingle between the shoulder blades'. For Nabokov the purity of aesthetic bliss, 'that little shiver behind is quite certainly the highest form of emotion that humanity has attained when evolving pure art and pure science'.[16]

This inspiring expression of the need to feel free I reiterate is not grounded in any 'moral source', and Nabokov distances this version of art from 'topical trash' like the work of Orwell, or Mann, which attempts to deal with morality in an explicit way. At the same time, Nabokov's talent for producing and appreciating authentic literature leads him to attribute to it a moral quality of his own (rather as did Charles Taylor in his own discussion of authenticity):

> The capacity to wonder at trifles – no matter the imminent peril – these asides of the spirit, these footnotes in the volume of life are the highest forms of consciousness, and it is in this childishly speculative state of mind, so different from common sense and its logic, that we know the world to be good.

For Nabokov this form of the good is a rare thing: an idiosyncratic capacity to be alive to the quotidian detail of life, and only available to 'a few thousand others' with a sufficiently 'childishly speculative state of mind'.

> When we perform that necessary mental twist which is like learning to swim or making a ball break, we realise that goodness is something sound and creamy, and beautifully flushed, something in a clean apron with warm bare arms that have nursed and comforted us.[17]

It is clear that in Nabokov there is something of the idolization of the child and child-like wonder that is supposed to give weight to the case – but this, I argue, is to be confused about what is admirable in children. It may be commonplace and perfectly reasonable to associate childhood with innocence and purity, but the moral implications of the conflation should be resisted. Like Emerson we are right to admire their unconquered eyes, but *pace* Nabokov, Taylor and Rousseau, literature has also shown us that there is no given link between the child and goodness. From *Lord of the Flies* to the Brazilian film *City of God*, we should learn to accept Conrad's prediction (in *The Heart of Darkness*) that, stripped of convention, there is no guarantee that a savage will be noble.[18]

For Richard Rorty, who shares the liberal view that 'cruelty is the worst thing we can do', knowing the good 'is just sensing what matters to other people'. And he contrasts this (where Nabokov conflates it) with the 'remorseless pursuit of the sort of ecstasy which necessarily excludes attention to other people'.[19] Watching a child play alone fills us with wonder, watching children playing together can make us wince, and reminds us that a capacity for empathy and imaginative identification is not their strong suit. As George Eliot commented in *Middlemarch*, 'we are all of us born in moral stupidity'. In the context of this chapter I argue with Rorty and against Nabokov that 'the pursuit of autonomy is at odds with feelings of solidarity'.[20]

The outstanding celebrant of freedom as self-creation was Nietzsche, who urged that we make our lives into works of art. 'We should learn from artists . . . we want to be the poets of our life – first of all in the smallest, most everyday matters'.[21] His madman famously declared that God is dead. With the death of God comes the death of the ultimate audience, omniscient and omnipresent. Consequently, posterity also loses its draw:

> who dares anymore to undertake works for whose completion one would have to count on millennia? For that basic faith is dying out on which one can count in that way, the faith on the basis of which one can make promises, anticipate the future in a plan: namely the faith that human beings have value, have meaning, only in so far as they are stones in a great construction – for which purpose they must be first of all stable 'stones'. And above all not actors!
>
> Briefly put – ah, it will be kept silent long enough! – what from now on will be no longer constructed, no longer can be constructed, is a society in the old sense of the word; we are lacking everything to build this construction – above all, the material. None of us is material for a society anymore – there's a truth that is timely![22]

The point for Nietzsche is that we must be *actors* in control of our destiny as opposed to being controlled by it, and not *stones*, mere tools in the hands of other actors. This is why we are no longer material for a society, we must admire the lightning flash of *becoming* rather than inertly *being*. We should stop being 'corner dwellers', but rather become the one who 'revels and delights in the opposite, in the unlimited, in the "free in itself"'.[23] Importantly, we see here how the need to feel free is opposed to the need to feel justified.

The ideal of breaking free has nothing to do with other people. Nietzsche asks 'how could we . . . still be content with the human beings of the present? This is too bad, but it is unavoidable that *when we look at their worthiest goals and hopes it is hard for us to keep a straight face . . .*' (emphasis added).[24]

So creativity can just as easily serve destructive or redemptive ends, and from this vantage-point even torture and art can begin to look alike. Rorty develops this Nietzschean idea by looking at the depiction of cruelty in George Orwell's *1984*. O'Brien, the intellectual member of Big Brother's Inner Party, dismantles Winston Smith's psychology to humiliate his 'worthiest goals and hopes' with all the care and creativity of Leonardo's inspired rendering of human anatomy.

> Torture is not for the sake of getting people to obey, not for the sake of getting them to believe falsehoods (like two plus two equals five). As O'Brien says, 'The object of torture is torture'. For a gifted and sensitive intellectual living in a post-totalitarian culture, this sentence is the analogue of 'Art for art's sake' or 'Truth for its own sake,' for torture is now the only art form and the only intellectual discipline available to such a person.[25]

William Faulkner echoes this theme:

> The writer's only responsibility is to his art. He will be completely ruthless if he is a good one. He has a dream. It anguishes him so much he must get rid of it. He has no peace until then. Everything goes by the board: honor, pride, decency, security, happiness, all, to get the book written. If a writer has to rob his mother, he will not hesitate; the *Ode on a Grecian Urn*

is worth any number of old ladies.[26]

So both Emerson and Nietzsche, near contemporaries on different continents, offer a conception of the free agent, what the political theorist Michael Sandel calls the 'unencumbered self'. And both do so in a bold exclamatory style, vividly raging. The distinctiveness of Emerson's picture is the seriousness he accords this stance as contrasted with Nietzsche's ironic detachment. Here we are witnessing the invention of authenticity, as contrasted with an invention of aesthetic sensibility. Emerson (like Thoreau or Whitman) is American – bold, strong and pursuing the truth however unpalatable it may be, while Nietzsche (like Proust or Nabokov) is European, playfully aiming at 'the great seriousness', at bliss. What they have in common is a celebration of freedom and a distrust of tradition. The traditionalists, the knockers, who feel threatened by either force react typically by seeing these champions of freedom as self-regarding narcissists; the American variant as spiritually navel-gazing or culturally materialistic, while the European version (especially Continental philosophy) is mocked for a nihilistic disregard for standards and the triumph of style over substance. This is the point though: moralists will always find a way to criticize an expression of the need to be free – the need is in itself amoral.

Sex, Death and the 'Search for Strange'

The need for freedom is, of course, not confined to adventurers, artists and intellectuals. As Taylor rightly points out, it lies at the heart of modern consciousness and permeates all who give it permission or acknowledgment (as well, I would argue, as those who do not). After Freud, who, according to Philip Rieff, 'democratized genius by giving everyone a creative unconscious', we cannot fail to register that these disruptive, creative urges (the psychological need to *feel* free) are in us all. In our permissive society the realm of sexual fantasy is clearly one where freedom has an important role to play.

In the movie *Internal Affairs*, Richard Gere is a corrupt cop who inflames the jealousy of the officer investigating him (Andy Garcia) by claiming that he is having an affair with Garcia's wife. Gere is lying, but Garcia is persuaded because he recognizes the plausibility in Gere's pronouncement that wives 'are all searching for strange', the provocative claim being that the hottest sex is illicit. Perversions, obsessions, the apparent mutability of the most mundane objects into the stuff of erotic fantasy, all remind us that the realm of eroticism is dominated by the need to walk on the wild side. So subversive of the moral order are these instincts that Freud propounded that civilization is built on their repression.

In the Company of Men, another misogynist film, features a sociopath called Chad who invents a vicious game co-opting Howard, his spineless friend and colleague. They decide to find a vulnerable woman (Christine, who is deaf), seduce her, convince her they love her and leave her humiliated. Howard is unable to carry it through but Chad never blinks; he can't stop laughing as he tells Christine, who has fallen in love with him by the end of the film, that it was all a game. At the height of her despair he stares into her eyes and, with barely restrained glee, asks 'How do you feel, right now?' He also engineers the destruction of Howard's career, and replies to the beseeching question *'Why?'* with 'Because I can'. His cruelty seems untroubled, and while Rousseau may echo our sentiments that 'the wretch has neither life nor feeling, he is already dead', Chad goes to sleep with a smile. You could argue that his cruel destruction of Christine and Howard was a work of art. Compare it to Richard Rorty's description of O'Brien's torture of Winston Smith:

Presumably Winston is only one of a long series of people, each with a mind like O'Brien's own, whom O'Brien has searched out, studied from afar, and eventually learned enough about to enjoy torturing. With each he has entered into a long, close, intensely felt relationship, in order at the end to feel the pleasure of twisting and breaking the special, hidden, tender parts of the mind . . .[27]

This is where the celebration of freedom can lead any of us, and there is nothing we can do to wish it away, or tame it as Rousseau or Taylor might try. The freedom urge is neither moral nor conventional. More important, in various forms it resides in us all, though it will never be recognized by some – by those who have so carefully manufactured their identity and denied the appeal of disruption or the search for strange (those who distrust the Enlightenment-bending interventions of Darwin and Freud). But their state of denial will not convince those of us who can't help recognize the urge to drive into oncoming traffic or to shout *'Fuck off!'* when asked a question by the boss. We are not the directors of a rational drama played out in our inner Cartesian theatre – we're twisted (crooked timber, in Kant's poetic phrase), and our yearning to subvert best-laid plans is why Douglas Hofstadter was right to bet 'you can't read this sentence without thinking of Agatha Christie':[28]

Far from behaving . . . with the regular intelligibility of a clock, the bent of the living and of man in particular is to MISbehave, in all senses of the word – from developing allergies, which make poison out of delicacies, to committing crimes which, as in saints and statesman, can later seem the highest wisdom. It is even proved by research that man must have his ration of dreaming, that is, of irregular and inaccurate thinking. These facts of experience require that any science of the regularities of behavior be always qualified and admonished by another discipline, a learned lore of misbehaviour.[29]

The freedom we seek is both positive and negative (in Isaiah Berlin's distinction). It is the freedom *to* . . . discover, create and fantasize, but equally importantly it is the freedom *from* . . . structure, schemes, codes and above all other people – freedom from the sources of security, and thus freedom is the opposite of justification. This is central to my claim. Our need to be free directly contradicts our need to feel justified. Justification, as I describe in the next chapter, is *all* about other people; freedom has nothing to do with them.

Of course, the ultimate freedom is death, the final escape. This idea can be found throughout the history of philosophy and literature. True to this theme, Freud posited that we are driven by a death instinct, Thanatos, as much as by Eros, the life instinct. Adam Phillips takes this thought a step further in his book *Darwin's Worms* to claim that death, suffering, loss and mourning are necessary to living properly. 'Beside the instinct to preserve living substance and to join it into ever larger units (Eros), there must exist a contrary instinct to dissolve those units and to bring them back to their primeval, inorganic state',[30] namely Thanatos. Freud often quoted Hamlet's 'use every man after his desert, and who should escape whipping?' or, as Phillips puts it, 'everyone deserves to be punished'. I take this to mean that while we all yearn for freedom, this yearning is, at its limit, destructive of all forms of justice, solidarity, people and 'their worthiest goals and hopes' – any judge (any audience) would have to punish such a yearning. This can be read as saying that the wish to die is an extreme form of the wish to be free – as a desire to experience the loss of structure and other people without which we can never be free. As Phillips glosses it, deprivation is the precondition for invention. It is only by experiencing the little death of tearing loss from comforting structure that we can do something shiny and new.

Freud (like Sartre) hated biography, and so (Phillips argues) invented the unruly death instinct to foil biographers. His daughter Anna Freud describes 'the death instinct or destructive force serving the opposite aim (from the life instinct) of undoing connections and destroying life'. The fact that we are always 'tampering with the evidence of ourselves'[31] is another way to restate the equation of Thanatos and freedom. It is an expression of the idiosyncratic need to be beyond the reach of description – the subversive attempt to break away from language. So at its limit, death is an object of desire, or, in Freud's words, 'the aim of all life is death'.[32]

For death to be an object of desire it is crucial for Freud that it is constructed *of our own fashion* – it is not enough to die, rather we must die on our own terms so that self-destruction is the ultimate act of self creation. Think of the endings of *Thelma and Louise* or *Butch Cassidy and the Sundance Kid*. Again, this is the essence of the need for freedom – to be a Nietzschean actor who steps out of the shadows, no longer a 'corner dweller', stepping, completely alone, into the light.

Freedom as the Escape from Language

Why do we feel uncomfortable when we hear people have been talking about us without our being present? One reason is that we have been turned into a topic of conversation; we have ceased to act and have turned into Nietzsche's despised, stable stone in someone else's construction. Richard Rorty describes the problem in a discussion of Proust and Sartre:

> [Proust] wanted to free himself from the descriptions of himself offered by the people he had met. He wanted not to be merely the person these others thought they knew him to be, not to be frozen in the frame of a photograph shot from another person's

perspective. He dreaded being, in Sartre's phrase, turned into a thing by the eye of the other.[33]

What Rorty is describing should not be confused with our need to avoid being misunderstood or falsely accused, but rather seen as a need to assert that there is something about being me that no-one else could ever understand, nor could I explain. This is presumably why Freud loathed biography. He was so alive to the preciousness of being an Actor, uniquely free, that he could not stand to be turned into a Nietszchean stepping-stone by others wishing to trap his lived life in words. Sartre very similarly insisted that historical biography makes no sense as a project – either you write what is true or you write an intelligible history – the one possibility excludes the other, for experience always tears free of convention. In remembering holidays, we don't re-experience them, but simply retell them through photos and diaries, and in the retelling we move away from the lived experience. In this sense words betray experience, or, as José Ortega y Gasset expressed it, 'to create a concept is to move away from reality'. Put this way, the need to be free is the need to flee from language. It is a need that is as powerful as it is ultimately self-defeating.

Freud invented the notion of repression to explain how we can push out of consciousness the mad desires of unfettered freedom, and in the process he made us all poets of our lives. In his book *Freudian Repression*, Michael Billig offers an explanation of how such repression gets done (something Freud omitted to supply). Billig's claim is that we need to look to language if we are to see the mechanism in action for 'language is fundamentally both expressive and repressive'.[34] Furthermore, if with Wittgenstein we accept that language permeates all aspects of human behaviour, it is important to see how the need for freedom expresses itself in the way we talk with others.

Billig outlines how the unspoken codes and norms that govern our conversation have tremendous force on what we can and cannot say:

> For instance, when speakers are coordinating their turns in dialogue, they must demonstrate that they are yielding and taking up the conversational space according to the requisite norms . . . Not only are there systems of turn-taking, but a host of other norms enable dialogue to take place . . . All language communities have codes for talking, together with ways of showing disapproval when such codes are infringed . . . If codes of talking are broken, not only is the immediate conversation threatened, but so is the cultural morality of social interaction.[35]

At the same time says Billig, 'one might suspect, following the logic of Freud's observation (that morality indicates the presence of desire), that dialogic constraint, practised as second nature, will evoke the countervailing desire to be conversationally free – to say what one will, to interrupt with abandon and so on.'[36]

Billig makes the point by explaining that every utterance carries the shadow of something not uttered.[37] An example he uses is how a mother teaching a child to be polite simultaneously teaches the child how to be rude. It is only by saying 'Don't say that!' that a child knows what to avoid saying if it is to be polite and so exactly what *to* say if it wants to subvert things by being rude. In learning language we learn the codes that we must obey to participate in human interaction, but we also learn to desire their subversion: 'temptation is created by the social conditions of constraint, as the existence of rules itself provokes the possibility of shameful desire.'[38]

In order to be a Nietzschean 'actor' or Emerson's 'unconquered' child we need to subvert codes indeed, but to do so in such a way as to help define new codes to share with the audience who appreciated the act of subversion. To turn Billig's argument back on itself, the desire to break rules leads back to the desire to make new rules. The ideal form of code breaking creates a new code that hangs in the air before being embraced by an appreciative audience, where shock turns into applause. Comedy, inspiration, charisma all have this heroic quality. All actors need their audiences, without whom they may as well be dead. Sometimes a stronger poet will look to the applause of future generations or to lots of little Nabokovs (Nabokov's ideal reader) so as to allow their abnormal discourse to create a new norm. Without that audience in mind, nothing has been created.

Conversation affords as many degrees of freedom as our imagination allows. Codes are ignored, broken or adhered to depending on the background knowledge and motives of the interlocutors. Wittgenstein once noted that 'in a conversation: one person throws a ball; the other does not know whether he is supposed to throw it back, or throw it to a third person, or leave it on the ground, or pick it up and put it in his pocket, etc.'[39] Good friends routinely invite each other to jump codes with them; only by knowingly breaking conversational codes in a way your friend can and will follow do you reinforce the significance of the relationship. In proper conversations the rules are laid down to be upended and replaced. The surest sign of a failing friendship is when conversations follow too easily the well-laid tracks of nostalgia and past experiences and never go somewhere new and delightful. Frankie, the narrator in Tim Lott's *White City Blue*, captures the fading friendship of his old schoolmates:

Not that it hadn't been great sometimes, and sometimes even now it was. But more and more it felt like history hadn't yet found its way into the past. Stuck right there in the present gumming everything up. You could tell because history is what our meetings – Colin, Tony, Nodge and me – are getting to be about. Not that great spontaneous rap, that impro, of irony and sub-irony and sub-sub-irony, and dry wind-up and piss-take, that you can do when you've tapped the vein that runs between you, that can have you doubling up with laughter and the joy of having mates – the illicitness of it, the crudeness of it, the wonderful little-boy playfulness of it. No, not that, but, like I say, history, the immediate and distant past. What have you done? Where have you been? What have you seen? How was X when you saw her? How was that match you went to? Do you remember when? Too much of that now. Too much.[40]

Banal rule-following may work when buying a train ticket, but it does not sustain a relationship worth having. At the same time you can't break all the conversational rules at once; that would be gibbering.[41] Intimacy demands we jump out of the code in a way that invites our partner to jump too. We break codes with a tease, an intimate revelation, an obscenity, some gossip, even a raised eyebrow or a smirk. Laughter is often the hallmark of increasing intimacy as the joke-teller takes a risk, breaks a code and is rewarded by laughter rather than contempt. The best conversations walk on a delightful tightrope, wobbling between madness and banality.

But of course once we accept that it is through language that we express our need to be free we co-opt the actual or potential interlocutor (the audience) into the process of expressing our freedom. This is the heart of the paradox. To be free is to break the codes of appropriateness, and yet our breaking those codes has a self-defeating logic to it – to be free is to look anew for justification. When my two-year-old daughter heads off into a new room with devilish intent, she sneakily looks back to see if I'm watching – there would be no point being naughty if I wasn't there.

I see all this as telling us that we are perpetually in conflict over intimacy. Intimacy comes from both succumbing and escaping. We succumb to others' invitations to escape, and by escaping offer our invitation in return. We can't have intimacy while playing safe. One setting designed for the most intimate of conversations is psychoanalysis, where free association requires that we break free of all conversational codes in front of the analyst – in itself a risky act of incredible intimacy. Phillips points out that 'free associating . . . is akin to mourning; it is a process of detachment that releases hidden energies'.[42] It is like dying, in that by cutting loose of the bonds of rational communication we become an inanimate piece of material, but crucially it is an act of our own making. We are not rendered inanimate by being turned into an object in the verbal snapshot of other people's conversation. On the contrary, we become inert by breaking free of describability. This way, paradoxically, Nietzsche's actor has become a stone in order to fall through language.

So to pursue freedom to its extreme, to the point where you are literally uninterpretable to others, is where madness or meaninglessness lies. The nub of the issue here is that it is only when someone else sees what you see that you know you are not mad. We constantly look back over our shoulders when heading to somewhere new with cues like 'Know what I mean?' 'Look, this may sound crazy, but . . .'. There are indefinite ways to be unique,[43] but only those ways that have meaning to an audience can be a significant expression of, and so satisfy our desire for, uniqueness. The paradox is that we want to express our desire for freedom by building our own horizons so that we know we are not a Nietzschean stone in someone else's construction. Yet when our vision is created we need someone else to see what we see, a suitable audience to applaud, or at least to vindicate, the creation.

This is in part the answer to modernity's knockers, to Robert Bellah's question 'How can we avoid sliding into the abyss?' For the way of 'overcoming the emptiness' of 'purely arbitrary values' is to recognize that there are no such things as 'arbitrary values'. All meaningful action is witnessed, in some sense, by an audience before whose judgement we must submit. We need audiences to judge our urge to be free, and we are audiences judging the freedom of others.

This need for an audience in itself leads to two dangers. If the applause is too easily achieved we worry about whether we have really been free after all (our banality damned by faint praise); on the other hand, instead of applause we may receive blank silence, or worse, a Nietzschean sneer 'at our worthiest goals and hopes'. Either outcome risks the terrible pain of humiliation. These fears can lead us to deny the importance of the audience in the first place – to deny the need for justification and to imagine our freedom as truly unencumbered. But this denial is self-deception, or 'bad faith' in Sartre's terms. The paradox of freedom is that it is worth nothing if it is not justified, and justification, as I argue in chapter Three, only really comes from other people. If our need for freedom paradoxically converts into our need for justification, then, to quote Bellah again, 'we never get to the bottom of ourselves on our own'.[44] Put in other terms, while the pursuit of happiness today revolves around answering the question *What do I really want?*, the question only makes sense in terms of its ancient moral counterpart *How ought I to live?* [45] This latter question is the subject of chapter Three.

While it took Sartre to show us that we are all 'condemned to be free', it was Simone de Beauvoir who showed the bankruptcy of the thesis of freedom without justification:

> the passionate man (or the nihilist, and other free people) inspires a certain admiration, he also inspires a kind of horror at the same time. One admires the pride of a subjectivity which chooses its end without bending itself to any foreign law and the precious brilliance of the object revealed by the force of this assertion. But one also considers the solitude in which this subjectivity encloses itself as injurious.[46]

Our search for freedom, when fully realized, makes us fit to become justified by our audiences, who in turn assert their freedom to judge, applaud, fantasize, invent us, so that, as de Beauvoir has it, 'man can find a justification of his own existence only in the existence of other men'.

CHAPTER THREE

Feeling Justified

If we can rely on each other, we need not rely on anything else
Richard Rorty

Sam Peckinpah's western *Ride the High Country* portrays two ageing lawmen, Gil Westrum and Steve Judd, who are contracted to escort and deposit gold from the mining town of Coarsegold to the bank in the valley below. Gil plans to steal the shipment and attempts to convince his long-time friend Steve to join the scheme, claiming it as just reward for all of the hard, underpaid years they had served. 'You know, Steve, the only things on a poor man's back when he dies are the clothes of pride, and they aren't any warmer to him dead than they were when he was alive. Is that all you want, Steve?' Steve contemplates briefly and replies, '*All I want is to enter my house justified.*'

The implicit question for Steve is, justified by what? Isn't Gil claiming to be justified too? Don't they *deserve* the gold after all their unappreciated years of service? What exactly is constraining Steve from joining Gil's plan? God, pride, friends, family, morality, fear or picturing the reflection of his own face in the mirror every morning? This chapter asks what we do when we have less reason than ever to impede ourselves from self-indulgence, while arguing that we cannot be happy if we live without being accountable. Feeling justified by others is the modern counterpoint to feeling free, and just as profound, subtle and complex a need. In fact, to be happy is to feel truly justified.

For most of our history, roughly from Aristotle to the Enlightenment, the notion of happiness was linked to virtue and the pursuit of the Good Life in a moral sense, which gave a clear formula for how we ought to live, i.e., how to feel justified. Then, as I explored in chapter One, morality seemed to be undercut by a feelgood factor, and in the process the topic of happiness moved from the province of philosophy to that of psychology. Many commentators, modernity's 'knockers', have felt that this loss of standards has left the subjective notion of happiness virtually empty of content, and yearn for a return to the days when we all knew our place in the order of things. Unfortunately for them, there is no way back to social mores and religious structures that once made our lives accountable. Once we tasted freedom we became addicted, and older moral codes look hopelessly unsuited to our times. The problem is that the structures have collapsed while the question they were designed to answer – *How should I live?* – persists.

The moralistic knockers have half a point. Freedom and self-expression alone are not sufficient to describe the content of happiness today. Freedom without constraint, as I have claimed, leads to meaninglessness, madness or death. Accountability has to re-enter the story, but in a way suited for our emancipated times. We need to understand why Steve's self-control still looks rational despite the norms of self-indulgence, and to account for the relevance of normative judgements like 'She says she's happy, but is she really?' Why not just use the word Morality rather than justification to explain this? I discuss this further below, but essentially the connotations of the word point to external sources of judgement – commandments, the done thing, the chain of being, etc. – which are almost bankrupt today. This objective standard has been replaced by our need for good opinion. The philosopher Rom Harré in his classic book *Social Being* observed that 'people have a deep sense of their own dignity, and *craving for recognition* as beings of worth in the opinions of others of their kind'. He goes further to make the remarkable assertion that the *pursuit of reputation* in the eyes of others is the overriding preoccupation of human life.[1]

There is nothing so fatal to our happiness than to have our yearning for justification unsatisfied. In 'Civilization and its Discontents' (initially entitled *Unhappiness in Culture*) Freud points out that

> our possibilities of happiness are already restricted by our constitution. Unhappiness is much less difficult to experience. We are threatened with suffering from three directions: from our own body, which is doomed to decay and dissolution and which cannot even do without pain and anxiety as warning signals; from the external world, which may rage against us with overwhelming and merciless forces of destruction; and finally from our relations to other men. The suffering which comes from this last source is perhaps more painful to us than any other.[2]

It is this third kind of suffering in which I am most interested. Rich Western societies have gone some way to ameliorating the effects of the first two, or at least can reduce our suffering on those fronts sufficiently to give us plenty of time to worry over the third. The first two forms of suffering are those that all sentient creatures face. The third is peculiarly human, and is capable of producing a very human form of pain – the excruciatingly private experience of humiliation. Happiness has two opposites, sadness and humiliation. While there are many obstacles to happiness, including physical pain, financial hardship, fear, obligation, boredom, oppression, it seems clear that the loneliness of humiliation, of shame or of rejection (as any sadist will know) are more opposed to happiness than anything else. For if feeling happy is to feel truly justified, then in the case of humiliation, where we feel so contaminated and quarantined, the possibility of happiness is excluded by definition.

In Tim Lott's *White City Blue*, Frankie, the narrator, fails to defend his closest friend, Colin, when set upon by the school bully, Tony. Tony, in a mocking imitation of Colin's alcoholic father, starts up:

> 'Ye na, ye ma son, and . . .' He threw his arms around Colin and pretended to cry. 'And I love ya, by Christ I do. But I just want just the one drink and I'll buy ya some fuckin stamps for ya birthday, och the fucking noo and hoots, you cunt, honest I will.'
>
> The laughter swelled into an ugly balloon. Colin, I knew well, collected stamps in lovingly tended albums. All the stamps were worthless, but he liked the colours and patterns and the ordering that could be achieved, by country, by colour, by price. As with his handwriting, it was a way for him to get to grips with a world that was falling out of control.
>
> Colin looked up. I felt a wrenching in my stomach as he caught my eye. I knew I had to do something, I even moved to do something. But I'd started to be a somebody instead of a nobody. And I didn't want to give it up . . .
>
> Something changed in Colin when he saw my face, when he saw what was in it – or to be more accurate, what was absent from it. He knew at that moment I wasn't going to help him, that the last thing in his life that he trusted had failed.

At some point in moving from 'unconquered' child to mature adult we learn about the pain of humiliation and deal with it in a variety of ways. Maybe it happens in the first few years when we reach out smiling to a parent who returns our affection with a slap.[3] Maybe, like Colin, we learn it at school. Maybe it comes from the generalized feeling of not being understood (which, like being falsely accused, is acutely isolating). Whenever it happens, we learn that there is just nothing worse. Some react by sealing off the feelings of need that bring with them the feelings of exposure. With many people (many men especially) the tactic, learned young and easily ingrained, is to look to more reliable, but ultimately unsatisfactory, sources of justification, such as stamp collecting.[4]

Freud enumerates a range of ways we avoid this kind of suffering, including becoming a hermit or taking up yoga to enjoy the 'happiness of quietness', sublimating instincts into getting pleasure from work (this he reserves mainly for artists and scientists), fantasy, imagination, escapism, as well as getting drunk or going mad.[5] These routes, rather than offering justification, are actually about the pursuit of freedom. They all involve some form of *turning away* from the world of other people. Freud offers an alternative that does not turn away:

> On the contrary, it clings to the objects belonging to that world and obtains happiness from an emotional relationship to them . . . [it] holds fast to the original, passionate striving for a positive fulfilment of happiness . . . I am of course speaking of the way of life which makes love the center of everything, which looks for all satisfaction in loving and being loved.

The problem, of course, is that to pursue love is to open up ourselves to the possibility of great pain if it is unrequited. To quote Freud further: 'we are never so defenceless against suffering as when we love, never so helplessly unhappy as when we have lost our loved object or its love'.[6]

Love is only the most magnified source of justification lying at one end of a continuum that includes affection, applause, approval, recognition, intimacy, respect, sympathy, trust, loyalty and understanding, among others. These forms of justification can only be provided by our audiences. Audiences are the ground to the figure of our identity. A proper audience can withhold justification as easily as offering it; as in a theatre or concert hall, they can cheer or jeer. To experience the lack of proper justification has its own continuum of emotion that ranges from embarrassment to humiliation.

Hell is Other People

So here is the difficulty. We know that other people can be the source of extreme pain and unhappiness while realizing that to be happy we need to feel justified in their eyes. Gold medals, Nobel or Booker prizes, lots of money, charity work, getting married, raising children, losing weight, going to church, achieving fame are among the routes to justification we covet to satisfy the need to feel good about ourselves. Beyond these big visible sources of justification lie the more subtle cues and codes that saturate (some would say generate) our sense of who we are. Our sense of pride, shame, love, self-esteem, appropriateness and belonging depend on how we imagine ourselves judged in the details of what we do and say. We are governed by an invisible web of expectations and finely balanced codes and rules. In occasional contexts, like the pressure not to be the first person to clap after a concert, we come to glimpse the silent, and usually concealed, power of others that permeates our identity.

The secretive nature of such power can offer false comfort. It enables us to sustain the illusion that we are islands of consciousness, with unvarnished, self-contained views of the world and other people. We pride ourselves on our independence and persuade ourselves that we can draw entirely on inner resources for our motivation, and that we are truly free agents. As I said before, this self-contained view, if inspiring, is clearly self-defeating.

The theorist of justification *par excellence* is the sociologist Erving Goffman. In his books (*The Presentation of Self in Everyday Life, Asylums* and *Stigma*) he has perceptively interpreted the way our sense of self is constituted in our interactions with others and our social roles. Our self-respect is achieved through micromanaging, whether consciously or unconsciously, the impressions other people have of us. He describes how our sense of an authentic unitary self does not sit behind our public performances, it is an outcome of such performances, 'a performed character . . . a dramatic effect'. Goffman's deft style of writing avoids the turgid abstractions of most social science and is perfectly suited (as it is for Proust) to teasing out these delicate secrets.[7]

> At middle-class American funerals, a hearse driver, decorously dressed in black and tactfully located at the outskirt of the cemetery during the service, may be allowed to smoke, but he is likely to shock and anger the bereaved if he happens to flick his cigarette stub into a bush, letting it describe an elegant arc, instead of circumspectly dropping it at his feet.[8]

Furthermore, we don't need our audience to be physically present to guide our behaviour. We adhere to standards of behaviour 'because of a lively belief that an unseen audience is present who will punish [our] deviations from these standards'.[9] The hearse driver would be compelled to drop the cigarette end at his feet regardless of whether he could be seen. Now, contrary to Goffman's analysis, these pressures aren't so overwhelming that we cannot override them in any one context. Consider our chances of self-respect and dignity that come from our ability to say things of ourselves to which others will assent.

We present ourselves and manage impressions with tremendous alacrity. We respond uneasily to compliments because we know the risk of humiliation that will come from taking seriously praise that was intended as a joke or test of our modesty. Goffman reminds us that every performance requires that we do plenty of 'backstage' work to keep our 'front' acceptable and appropriate to our various audiences. We know instinctively how to impress the relevant audience.

The techniques of impression management are complex and dynamic attempts to balance credibility and reputation. Say, for example, you want to appear intellectual. The simplest way is to convey the idea that your tastes are *always* intellectual tastes. Your choice of books, music and art are all to be applauded as 'serious'. The safest way to maintain this identity without risk of the part being undermined is the spare and disciplined route of only indulging in serious activities – in this case there is no contrast between backstage and front-stage. If you allow yourself more humdrum pleasures, such as thrillers, football and pop music, you then have to engage tactically. The first tactic is to conceal evidence of these non-serious tastes. You have to hide the incriminating evidence backstage. In this scenario your intellectual performance runs the risk of being undermined by a single humiliating discovery (caught backstage, *flagrante delicto*, watching 'Who Wants to be a Millionaire?').[10] The less-risky tactic is to hedge, to reveal selective unserious pleasures, revelling in kitsch, say, with a knowing irony to convey the trustworthiness of your other, more-serious claims. Offering glimpses of backstage work helps maintain the credibility of your front-stage performance. But then you may worry that your equally knowing audience will spot your distancing irony for the warranting tactic it is, and so reveal a different level of back-stage machinery.[11] Another tactic is to be candid, to indulge your trivial pursuits without irony, thus maximizing the impression of genuineness. Of course, then you run the risk of diluting the front-stage performance to such a degree that the intellectual tag no longer fits. We can make these calculations in an instant, effortlessly, while barely conscious of the fact.

Front-stage versus backstage is not dishonesty versus sincerity. While it is right to note 'the tangled web we weave, when we practice to deceive', the web looks no less tangled when we communicate the truth. It is not enough to be helplessly honest, we need to be *convincing* – truth will not out by itself. For Goffman the skills of deception are exactly the skills of putting on any good performance. Integrity is not the issue. The honest performance and the cynical performance work with the same logic, for, as Auden put it, 'sincerity is technique'. This unsettling juxtaposition lies at the heart of my argument in this book.

Further complexity arises where there is no tactful mechanism with which to avoid distinct audiences coming together. The British BBC Radio 4 programme *Desert Island Discs* poses just this problem. (Each week a person of some fame or repute is invited to select the pieces of music he or she would want if marooned on a desert island, and, in the course of choosing and playing, ties them to episodes in his or her past life.) To participate requires personal choices to be made in public, forcing the show's guest to decide on one version of him- or herself while competing self-descriptions swim into view. In an article describing just this experience, Robert McCrum, the *Observer*'s literary editor, captured the difficulties well.[12] He described the insistent advice of colleagues and friends ('you must take Wagner'), and dwelled on the internal struggle regarding whom he was going to project. Would it be McCrum the intellectual, the aesthete, the dreamy idealist, the with-it rocker, or is it his more sentimental side? But in the course of this, 'I began to lose my sense of who I really was'. His difficulty came from the fact that the range of personae he would normally select from to put on stage, according to the audience for that occasion, were suddenly all visible together, jostling for approval, with no backstage to which he could retreat. McCrum struggled to decide who to be when determining which audience it mattered most to him to impress.

> We may practically say that he has as many different social selves
> as there are distinct *groups* of persons about whose opinion he

cares. He generally shows a different side of himself to each of these different groups.[13]

The challenge to our character, and the preservation of integrity, comes from maintaining a coherent self in the face of an audience that endures over time and not for just one performance.

Justified by What or Whom?

Our sources of justification come from a huge array of audiences – from work, from family, from friends and from enemies. If we look more closely, it becomes clear that the kinds of justification we aspire to divide into at least two forms. We seek acceptability in the light of two classes of audience: the audience made up of people and the more abstract audience provided by standards of excellence. This distinction is marked in practice by what we might call the pursuit of human versus non-human goals.

Non-human goals involve the pursuit of a neutral standard by which we can succeed or fail. A marathon runner I know captured it beautifully with his mantra 'The stop watch doesn't care about your ego'. For some athletes the goal can be clear and reliable, as it is for those who use their bank balance as their standard. More subtle, but equally non-human goals are the big abstract concepts much admired by intellectuals, artists and the religious. These are what the philosopher Hilary Putnam called 'God's-eye points of view'. They include Posterity, Truth, Morality, Perfection, Beauty – and God, of course. The pursuit of these goals has a venerable history. They were indeed once a source of justification, and submitting to their stringent demands can be intensely pleasurable and enriching. The psychologist Mihalyi Csikszentmihalyi describes the state of 'flow' that comes from being so engrossed in an activity we lose our sense of self. To induce flow, the activity has to balance between anxiety and boredom by being hard enough to keep us interested but not so hard as to make us give up. These goals can offer brutal tests of character and talent, yet when they are surmounted they can be the source of deep pleasure.

Despite the evident benefits of pursuing non-human goals, I believe they do not provide us with a true sense of justification. They are, strictly speaking, forms of 'turning away' from people, and turning away has become a less-effective source of true justification ever since the rise of the subjective individual; and now more than ever. This, I realize, is a controversial opinion. Many would say that a great artist can feel truly justified by creating a painting, an engineer by building a bridge or an athlete by winning a gold medal, and, rightly, that the rewards of obsessive engagement with the non-human have led to the most sublime achievements of human history. But the importance of these non-human goals in modern psychology is in their satisfaction of our need to feel free rather than our need to feel justified. If we are prodigiously talented we may allow ourselves to be judged by Posterity or The Truth; if less talented, there is always the world's largest beer-mat collection or the highest score in a video game, but the reason these offer no true justification in themselves is precisely that they are non-human and so have a neutral, indifferent gaze. While we can fail by these non-human standards, we can never be rejected or laughed at by them. Only those who have the power to humiliate you have the power to applaud you, and so if we protect ourselves from the possibility of being humiliated, we seal ourselves off from the possibility of being borne up by admiration. Of course we may, in the pursuit of these non-human goals, achieve applause and recognition and so feel properly justified. My point is that non-human goals cannot secure that end in themselves.

If we are to be happy, we must reconcile ourselves to our need for human sources of justification and accept their potency. We should believe Richard Rorty's assertion that 'if we can rely on each other, we need not rely on anything else'. In searching for justification, we are searching for applause. This is an extremely painful claim to accept. To crave applause is humiliating. Who wants to admit that without feeling accepted by an intimidating audience we cannot feel completely happy with ourselves? Worse still, being seen to be doing backstage work to gain applause is the best way to ensure you won't get it. We will never satisfy our need for justification by pursuing it, and we must not be craven if we seek to be happy.

Human versus non-human is a difficult distinction to keep in view. As I mentioned earlier, sometimes apparently non-human pursuits are all about expressing a need for human comfort. While my marathon running friend may be an exemplar of the pursuit of a non-human standard,[14] he may just as well have taken up athletics to search for approval from people that mattered, and thus humanized the goal. We cannot judge, just by looking, whether he is running away from, or running towards, other people. The same can be said for other private pursuits, such as writing, gambling, collecting, playing chess, listening to music, etc. These apparent candidates for non-human goals can easily be motivated principally by our desire to maintain or enhance our reputation, or to increase our chances of being loved. In that context they serve as human goals. By the same token there are public, human goals, which can be construed as a form of 'turning away'. These are goals that are constituted by real or imagined groups of people who have been abstracted out into another neutral standard. The Deserving Poor, Human Rights, Women's Lib, or the imaginary 'little nabokovs' envisioned by the actual Nabokov as his ideal readers. These goals and ideals may only form an audience in the most abstract sense; they are false gods from the point of view of true justification, and have no more leverage concerning our feelings of approval than do truth, posterity and tape measures.

We cannot reliably distinguish human from non-human goals in general terms. To know what kind of goal we are pursuing is to understand what *use* we make of goals – tools to help us feel justified or to help us feel free; connectors or disconnectors. This diagnosis is obviously not helped by the fact that the ability to connect properly (rather than submissively) is inextricably linked to the ability to disconnect.

In a recent interview with Susan Sontag we can see in her life an oscillation from the pole of justification to freedom and back again. The interviewer describes how Sontag turned away from the hope of love from her mother and stepfather and reached instead for non-human academic goals, before returning to human goals in the end:

> So what do you do as a bright young girl, who in her early teens, finds herself in the wrong place and misunderstood. Because how could this fatuous, inept guy [her step-father] ever understand her? Or, indeed, her mother – the 'cold, cruel woman' she describes. I think two things happen. You bypass adolescence . . . and *you find yourself a new authority* . . . She found it in academia. She says that books became her refuge. (emphasis added)

The interviewer goes on to point out that Sontag has recently found this new authority insufficient and has now renounced her non-human goals for the human variety – for friendship.

> It's not an easy quality to come by, this friendship, it requires a certain openness of character, and intrepidity of spirit. You read Sontag's early work, and it lies flat and lifeless on the page. Insightful, analytically intelligent it may be. But there is no friendship in it. She knows it and it makes her sad, or anyway rueful. 'What did I think I was doing?' – her most important talent she now says is as 'a great faller in love. A great adorer . . .'.[15]

But it is a thin line that separates 'a great adorer' from a big soppy fool. Our conscience is populated by our potent human audiences, not false gods, and courage is needed not to be craven in the face of their potency. The urge to be free is an expression of a need to render these audiences impotent. On occasion our defences are unexpectedly breached. Think of the children's song *Two Little Boys*, which starts as a childish nursery rhyme with wooden horses and play and yet with one line moves directly into 'Did you think I would leave you dying / When there's room on my horse for two?' For a child with her 'unconquered eye' the line is equivalent to any other in the song. For the adult who has been jagged by the pain of rejection and humiliation, it strikes a deeper chord. But we have to be careful in how we communicate our response, if we are not to be deemed soppy fools. Often we will admit this breach of our emotional defences only by skilfully deploying rhetoric that protects us against the accusation of naïveté: 'Extraordinary', we might remark, quoting Noel Coward, 'how potent cheap music is'. If we are less Cowardly, we can take a bigger risk ('this song always makes me cry') and thus receive even warmer applause or hoots of derision depending on how our performance is judged.

Audiences that Matter

If our conscience is crammed with the opinions of people who matter to us, it is very hard to accept our need for their approval. It is easy to recoil from our desire for acceptance and to take bold comfort in announcing that 'I don't need anybody' or 'It only matters to be true to yourself', or to take refuge in God's-eye points of view or abstract standards. The alternative is equally problematic in that if we are craven we are doomed never to receive the applause we crave. We can only be worthy of applause once we have succeeded in overcoming our need for it.

So who gets to make up our audience? We are very good at shielding ourselves from conscious acknowledgment of who populates the audiences that matter. Sometimes, as when we feel envious, we can catch dark glimpses of those crowding into our souls. The members of our audiences become clearer when we ask ourselves basic questions – Am I good, brave, honest, talented . . .? To answer honestly we must conjure up those we would need to persuade for these things to be true. The same goes for more negative assessments. Am I cruel, dishonest, cowardly, stupid, lazy . . .? Here the power of the audience comes out in the pain of recognition, or in the refusal to accept the verdict ('What the hell do they know?', 'I'll show them', 'They'll miss me when I'm gone' . . .).

Audiences are not easily altered, but neither are they a homogenous influence. Certain people become more salient in my mind when I engage in different activities. They may be defined by a structural relationship. The boss at work or the lover usually (though not always) loom large. Audiences may contain people we know whom we consider more successful, intelligent, attractive, witty and famous or just the people who know enough about our past to unpick a carefully woven public image. We do not choose our audiences, and if we are honest we realize that they include people we would be ashamed or fearful to admit. They are unreliable too. Liking you is not enough to qualify a friend as member of your audience – justifying audiences are not made up of adoring fans. In fact, adoring fans are almost never in our audience; they are too easy to please. Bertrand Russell once observed that he would rather have his ideas defended by his fiercest professional critic than by his closest friend 'innocent of philosophy'. George Eliot caught this feature of a proper audience in her depiction in *Middlemarch* of the love between Fred Vincy and Mary Garth:

'The theatre of all my actions is fallen,' said an antique personage when his chief friend was dead; and they are fortunate who get a theatre where the audience demands their best. Certainly it would have made considerable difference to Fred at that time if Mary Garth had had no decided notions as to what was admirable in character.[16]

If you lose the love or admiration of a member of your audience, their potency, far from vanishing, usually increases. They are still there, bearing witness, which is why the erstwhile provider of happiness – friend, colleague, lover, parent – so often becomes the provider of unhappiness.[17]

Morality and Character

The history of happiness outlined in chapter One is the story of the loss of traditional morality in the account of the good life. My focus on justification has a certain, subtle relationship to the role played by traditional morality that bears some examination. While we cannot reintroduce these lost, objective standards to counterbalance the feel-good factor, we must recognize that morality has not vanished, it has evolved. Far from disappearing, contemporary morality has been *privatized* and *localized* – it has come down to earth.[18]

While the search for justification and applause has little to do with traditional morality, the potent and enduring audience steps in as our source of private morality. The construction *privatized morality* seems oxymoronic in that morality is by definition an external set of standards, and so cannot be private. Some would say, for this reason, that morality is the wrong word. I think this is a mistake. Morality even in this subjective internalized sense is no less an organizing principle of a self-respecting life.[19]

We are guided in our behaviour and stance towards the world by what Rorty calls our 'vocabulary of moral reflection'. By this he means 'a set of terms in which one compares oneself to other human beings. Such vocabularies contain terms like magnanimous, a true Christian, decent, cowardly . . .'.[20] The key issue here is that in contemporary Western culture, moral reflection has become a question of character and conscience – as opposed to the mannered protocols of virtue and the public good. Moreover, this conscience of ours is not an abstract moral engine, it is populated by audiences of those whose respect, admiration and love we desire. Our sense of self is constituted in part by how we consider ourselves to be perceived by our audiences. As the philosopher Annette Baier puts it, 'one has to enter into one's own breast but also to listen for others' verdict'.[21]

A traditional rejoinder would be that this privatized morality can have no reliable grip on our behaviour and self-image if it is not anchored in a more solid foundation, something that transcends the mere judgement of other people. If morality has been privatized and is part of a personal project, the implication is that we are then free to tinker with our character – moral choices are up for grabs. This is a familiar critique of all forms of relativism, although it has never been a good argument. Even though a privatized view of morality lifts us off hooks and frees us of anchors, we are still stuck to a large extent with our audiences and our character. Changing either, though never ruled out in principle, would be painful and slow. To recognize the contingency of our deepest beliefs is one thing; to say that they therefore become optional is something completely different. I recognize that my love for my mother is rooted in a particular culture and history that would have been otherwise had I been adopted at birth and brought up in Kansas. But now she is part of my identity, I cannot discard her from my audience on a whim. We cannot shrug off our audiences, much as we might like to.

Richard Sennett in his *Corrosion of Character* draws on the French theorists Emmanuel Levinas and Paul Ricoeur to flesh out the notion that our conscience is populated by audiences. Levinas, he suggests, reminds us that fidelity to oneself (*'constance à soi'*)

> has a social dimension, in terms of being responsible to other people. This is at once a very simple and a complicated notion. Simple because it asserts [that] my sense of self worth depends on whether others can rely upon me. Complicated because I need to act responsibly, even if I do not know myself, and no matter how confused or indeed shattered my own sense of identity . . .
>
> No matter how erratic one's life, one's word must be good. But Ricoeur argues that we can hew to this standard only by imagining constantly that there is a witness to all we do and say, and that, moreover this witness is not a passive observer, but someone who relies upon us. In order to be reliable, we must feel needed; for us to feel needed, this Other must be needy. [22]

This Other (the audience) is made up of the eyes of people who influence us and, importantly, are not simply of our choosing. What is more, they may be needy as well as powerful. As the extract from *White City Blue* indicates, while Frankie was obviously Colin's treacherous audience, the haunting presence of Colin was an equally accusing audience for Frankie for years to come.

On the whole, the people who know us best are those who have the power to hurt us or make us feel ashamed. Strangers can certainly make us feel embarrassed, but they can rarely make us feel humiliated (*pace* the torturer).[23] Usually, the 'comfort of strangers' is all about the limits of their power over us; they can't get anywhere near as close as the knowing audience (they know nothing of our less-visible stigmata). A professional musician will tell you that it can be more nerve-wracking playing at a friend's wedding than at the opera house. Why would this be? After all, the wedding guests are on your side, in a way that a critical public will never be. The reason is that the musician cannot bask in the comfort of strangers at a wedding, and is necessarily exposed as needy. He or she knows, as Ricouer puts it, that 'because someone is counting on me, I am accountable for my action before another'. The bad news for those who have become so addicted to the comfort of strangers that they render everyone a stranger, is that they consequently deplete their chances of happiness – they have turned to non-human goals. Only those with the power to shame you have the power to make you happy.

The Persistence of Language

Our urge to be free I described in the previous chapter as an urge to escape language and interpretability. Freud's loathing of biography, or Sartre's refusal to be turned into a thing by the eye of another, exemplify this feature. This urge is bold but doomed, in that the only way to break free of language and meaning is madness or death. If we are to be inter-pretable as human, as rational, let alone admirable, we are condemned to ceaseless participation in Wittgenstein's 'language games', and so are perpetually in the process of seeking and providing justifying narratives. The self-descriptions we place on ourselves only hold up if we can get others to assent to them. As Adam Phillips puts it:

> we work very hard to keep versions of ourselves in other people's minds; and, of course, the less appealing ones out of their minds. And yet everyone we meet invents us, whether we like it or not. Indeed nothing convinces us more of the existence of other people, of just how different they are from us, than what they can make of what we say to them. Our stories often become unrecognisable as they go from mouth to mouth . . .[24]

As Wittgenstein reminds us, the comforting thought of a private language, in which we can take refuge, is illusory; we can only make use of descriptions of ourselves that can be held up to view in front of others and attempt to control their 'versions' to ensure we experience respect rather than contempt.

Rorty's chilling and perceptive description of O'Brien's torture of Winston Smith gives this point the clarity of an extreme case. 'O'Brien wants to cause Winston as much pain as possible, and for this purpose what matters is that Winston be forced to realize that he has become incoherent. *Realize that he is no longer able to use a language or be a self.* (emphasis added). Rorty develops this thought by identifying our sense of self with the sentences we assert or believe.

> People can, their torturers hope, experience the ultimate humiliation of saying to themselves, in retrospect, 'Now that I have believed or desired *this* I can never be what I hoped to be, what I thought I was. The story I have been telling myself about myself – my picture of myself as honest, or loyal, or devout – no longer makes sense.[25]

For Winston Smith it was being faced with his utter phobia, rats, that got him to say the unforgiveable words 'Do it to Julia'. Torture and humiliation are an extreme case of the cruel presence of other people (or 'Hell' as Sartre calls them), but they stand at one end of a range that contains both the embarrassment of falling over in public and the agony of unrequited love. 'One is exposed to the other as a skin is exposed to what wounds it, as a cheek is offered to the smiter', as Levinas says, and so as soon as we step out of the comfort of 'corner dwelling' we are jolted by a sense of risk.[26]

But of course if we never take these risks, never confront an intimidating audience, we will never feel truly justified, never feel happy. The happiness gurus who talk about building self-esteem often advocate giving and receiving of 'affirmations' as though uncritical praise will 'heal our pain'. But unless the praise is earned it can never properly satisfy our yearning for approval. We can no more feel proud of irrelevant or insincere compliments than a comedian can enjoy canned laughter. A worthy audience must be *potent* in our eyes, with the power to rebuke. It can patronize, laugh at (as opposed to with), intimidate, reject, judge, embarrass, accuse, emotionally blackmail us and hurt our feelings. In its presence we are always exposed to the possibility of the humiliating sneer, the shame of betrayal or the pain of being misunderstood. Applause from a potent audience is sheer joy.

Feeling Justified Leads Back to Freedom

Erving Goffman points out a difficulty with justification that I have alluded to at various points. Our 'face', he says, 'is only on loan to [us] from society'; 'approved attributes and their relation to face make of every man his own jailor; this is a fundamental social constraint even though each man may like his cell'.[27] In striving for acceptability we become trapped by the consequent diminishing of our uniqueness.

The cell of normality may be comfortably padded, but it by itself is not enough for happiness; the thirst for justification is not that easily quenched. Once stern judges turn into adoring fans they lose their power to justify us – the club we wanted to be part of, now impotent, becomes a padded cell. While those defined as 'sub-normal' yearn to be accepted as 'normal' (like the South African 'coloureds' during the apartheid years who used to 'go for white'), the normals once accepted as such must strive for, fantasize about, admission to the next club, the 'super-normal' club. This is where the urge to be free comes into the search for true justification. To be truly justified we need to prove that our face is not on loan to us, but is of our own devising and so excellent as to be applauded by those whose good opinion we must not be seen to crave. We must strive to attain the oxymoronic status of accepted uniqueness as expressed in Groucho Marx's remark that he would never join a club that would accept him as a member. This is why club culture alone, the comfort of belonging, can never be a route to happiness. Club members are either anxious, barely qualified and terrified of being disqualified, or on the cusp of joining an even more exclusive club and feeling bored and trapped by the comforting prison of their current membership – the same goes for all clubs whether formal or informal; a family, a work setting, Goffman's asylum or the Groucho Club. The urge to be free is the heroic urge to render all our potent audiences impotent. This can only happen by trading our impotent audience for a more potent one, and we are never so worthy of applause than when we express this urge to be free of its appeal.

If we look at any kind of club closely enough, according to Goffman, 'we find a multitude of homely little histories, each in its way a movement of liberty. Whenever worlds are laid on, underlives develop.'[28] The sources of justification breed the need to break free, for if they do not, 'thus conscience does make cowards of us all'.[29] The counterpoint to conscience is courage, just as the counterpoint to justification is freedom. Justification can make us conscientious but craven, and freedom can make us bold but unaccountable; we are equally damned if we pursue either one without the redemptive force of the other. The problem of experiencing true justification is that we can only get it by bravely denying our need for it. Happiness isn't a destination; it's a retreat from security and an advance towards risk, while being a retreat from risk and an advance towards security – a perpetual oscillation. That is why happiness is paradoxical.

So the need to feel justified like the need to be free has two sides. It expresses itself both in the *yearning* for intimacy, approval, applause . . .

and in the *fear* of humiliation, rejection and shame. In order to satisfy the yearning we need to overcome the fear, to be brave enough to assert our freedom, our uniqueness, without which there is nothing to applaud. As Adam Phillips puts it, 'sometimes we suffer most by being unwilling to suffer enough'. That is to say, we suffer the pain of disconnection, disapproval or contempt by failing to take the brave risk of breaking free of the audience.[30]

How does this work? As outlined in the previous chapter, the mechanism of generating intimacy comes from breaking codes; literally exposing oneself to condemnation and applause by stepping onto the stage. Code breaking is disruptive; like tripping up in public, it throws us (either accidentally or voluntarily) onto the stage, into the light. Great comedy comes from resolving these disruptions (switching from being laughed at to being laughed with) and great heroism comes from saving the accidentally and helplessly exposed from humiliation – saving them from dying on stage.

Conclusion

The reason that the film *It's a Wonderful Life* provides the archetypal 'happy ending' is that it depicts true justification in the face of an intimidating audience and unjust accusations. After Clarence (the Angel) replays the life of the town without him, George Bailey (James Stewart) sees the difference his life has made to people. Even though his fairy-tale goodness goes unappreciated by the townspeople (and crucially by himself), at the end of the film they sacrificed (they gave money) to save him. Not only did the townspeople have the power to hurt him, he experienced their rejection and abuse throughout the film. He continued to make his own, free choices and had no sense of his own perceived value. The fact that vindication came from the abusers is precisely the source of the ending's power:

When a person . . . commits himself in a serious way to a claim or request and leaves himself no way out should this be denied by the audience, he usually makes sure that his claim or request is the kind that is likely to be approved and granted by the audience. If his motivation is strong enough, however, he may find himself making a claim or an assumption which he knows the audience may well reject. He knowingly lowers his defences in their presence, throwing himself, as we say, on their mercy. By such an act the individual makes a plea to the audience to treat themselves as part of his team or to allow him to treat himself as part of their team. This sort of thing is embarrassing enough, but when the unguarded request is refused to the individual's face, he suffers what is called humiliation.[31]

What Goffman fails to see by focusing on caution is that when he is accepted rather than refused, having taken the biggest risk, his elation is unequalled. This triumph over adversity is the hallmark of all happy endings. In fact the guarded performance is hardly a performance at all, since it removes, in the same act of caution, the possibility of insult and genuine acclaim. The more guarded we are, and are seen to be, the more we hide in the dark and the less worthy are we of true applause. The less guarded we are, the more we risk rejection and humiliation.

If we stay hidden in the audience we can never feel applauded, so we have to take the Levinassian risk of *saying*; we have to risk being slapped in the hope of being kissed. A performance must be unguarded or free enough to be worthy of a true reaction from an audience – either cheering or jeering. If it is too guarded then it is not a true performance and can only receive canned laughter; 'it seems that there is no interaction in which the participants do not take an appreciable chance of being slightly embarrassed or a slight chance of being deeply humiliated. Life may not be much of a gamble but interaction is.'[32] To be happy we need our brave risks to pay off.

Without the approval of our fellow humans we cannot be happy – but we can never enjoy approval, intimacy, love or applause without taking the risk of being free from such craven desires.

CHAPTER FOUR

Love

Do you believe in love at first sight? Most people I've asked answer '*No.*' And then, tellingly, 'It depends what you mean by love.' Most of us accept lust at first sight, but consider love to be a different matter. The minority who answer '*Yes*' invariably claim, like Christians, the revelation of direct experience. Love at first sight makes us queasy. It suggests a juvenile inability to distinguish 'true love' from infatuation; a Disneyesque convention, touted by sickly poets and troubadours. It's just not very grown up. Yet love at first sight is not as easy a target as it seems. In our image of love we still carry the ancient Greek picture (from Aristophanes) of humans as starfish-shaped creatures with four arms and four legs, split in two by angry gods, endlessly searching around for their complementary 'other half', the true lover that fate has preordained. How often do we hear that 'He just wasn't my type', or 'She's still looking for Mr Right'? The classic line in the movie *Jerry McGuire* – 'You complete me' – perfectly states the case. Despite our caution, we routinely imply, dare to hope, that our soulmate is 'out there' waiting to be found, like treasure. The early nineteenth-century essayist William Hazlitt, writing of Petrarch's love for Laura, offers one of a million such descriptions.

For the purposes of inspiration, a single interview was quite sufficient. The smile which sank into his heart the first time he ever
beheld her, played round her lips ever after, the look with which
her eyes first met his, never passed away.[1]

In fact, the question 'Do you believe in love at first sight?' forces us to
confront our anxiety about love in general. We may caricature the idea as
ridiculous, but isn't love, after all, ridiculous by its nature, whether at first
sight or otherwise? The very phrase *falling* in love underlines the feeling of
helplessness. Whether eyes meet across a crowded room, or passion stirs
after a respectable period of time, falling is hard to do with dignity. The
caveat 'It depends what you mean by love' is really asking 'do you mean wet,
sad, needy, clingy, *stupid* love, or grandly passionate, heroic, cool and sexy,
true love?' The problem being that *stupid* love and *true* love feel exactly the
same. They both involve the sensation of falling – the difference is only
whether you fall into someone's arms or flat on your face.

What is Love?

I am concerned in this chapter with what might be called 'adults only' love,
which ranges from romantic love to loving relationships; from falling in
love to being in love. I am not thinking here, except by way of contrast,
about our love of friends, family, pets, landscapes or jobs. I'm talking about
the stuff that unites poets and pop singers. The sociologist Francesco
Alberoni has described it like this:

being in love is the search for one's own destiny . . . a search for
one's own self, to the very bottom. This is achieved through the
other person, in dialogue with her, in the encounter where each
person seeks recognition in the other, in accepting, in under-

standing, in the confrontation and liberation of what was and of what is.[2]

How does this experience of love exemplify the paradox of happiness? I argue that we have always been capable of love, but that in recent times we've fallen in love with love because it promises to make us feel perfectly free *and* perfectly justified. Love as freedom is about self-expression, originality, feeling new-born, while love as justification is about intimacy, applause and recognition. These needs are in tension with each other – more, they are paradoxically linked in that the expression of the one instils the need for the other. Before I explore this ambivalence further, I need to provide some theoretical context and to say more about how love is a universal but culturally shaped desire. How love in our dreams and language today is both something very old and very new.

A perennial question for academics is whether love is a recent social construct or a deep human need that transcends time and culture. The universalists in their crudest form are represented by reductive evolutionists who tie love down to sex and reproduction. They focus on the differential investment that men and women make in producing a child and use this to explain why women are choosy nurturers who are chased in seduction games and men are promiscuous seed spreaders who do the chasing (though Stephen Beckerman's recent *Multiple Fathers* argues how well adapted promiscuity can be for women, countering the traditional sociobiological take in its own terms). But the oversimplification in this picture hardly needs stating – it is enough to pick a poem depicting love to step beyond its explanatory reach, such as this stanza from 'Love Without Hope' by Robert Graves:

Love without hope, as when the young bird-catcher
Swept off his tall hat to the Squire's own daughter,
So let the imprisoned larks escape and fly
Singing about her head, as she rode by.

While a deterministic line takes little account of the rich complexity of our erotic life, this crude evolutionary explanation clearly has some merit. In so far as love is connected to sexual desire at all, we cannot exclude Darwin from the story. Sexual desire is as close to a universal cross-cultural feature of the human condition as you can get. Yet it is equally clear that eroticism goes far beyond the original procreative urge underpinning sexual desire. As the sociologist Zygmunt Bauman points out, in our reproductive endowment nature takes no chances by massively oversupplying sexual energy, capacity and desire in relation to that needed for the mere continuation of the species. Eroticism, says Bauman, 'is about recycling that waste'.[3] That is to say, this surplus capacity must be redirected in its search of satisfaction through cultural outlets. Societies have historically managed this tension by connecting eroticism to sex (where love has nothing to do with it, and eroticism is a mere proxy for the need to procreate) or connecting it to love (where sex is made illicit and eroticism is validated by the ideals of romance).

The main argument that undermines the crude evolutionary account is the irrational quality of true love. There are so many ways in which people have damaged their chances of procreative success by falling madly in love with someone unattainable (like Graves's bird-catcher), that the deterministic model has to be severely questioned. As the anthropologist Charles Lindholm asks: 'Why should the choice of a mate be surrounded by a cloud of romance? Why don't men simply choose the best gatherer, the most fecund child-bearer? Why do women not automatically select the male most likely to bring down the prey?'[4]

Love and foolishness are forever associated; we rush in where we should fear to tread. In a piece of bravura speculation, Stephen Pinker offers a remarkable evolutionary account of how head-over-heels love can come to override the best advice. His account does better justice to the universal but irrational (and thus unpredictable) qualities of love than his less subtle evolutionary confrères. Given that, as Pinker believes, we are normally rational optimizers looking for reproductive success, the logic governing my search for a mate is to find the most attractive (financially, physically, socially, etc.) who would settle for me:

> Somewhere in the world of five billion people there lives the best-looking, richest, smartest, funniest, kindest person who would settle for you. But your dreamboat is a needle in a haystack, and you may die single if you wait for him or her to show up . . . At some point it pays to set up house with the best person you have found so far.[5]

And so far so familiar for the crude evolutionists – this just looks like yet more sociobiology. But Pinker is clearly no determinist, since he argues that this rational calculation leaves your partner extremely vulnerable: 'The laws of probability say that some day you will meet a more desirable person, and if you are always going for the best you can get, on that day you will dump your partner.' So why should your partner (or you for that matter) ever commit in the first place?

Pinker speculates that this is why romantic love evolved. It works as a guarantee that the person who has settled for you has not done so tactically, thereby ready to dump you when 'a ten out of ten moves in next door'. They chose you because they have fallen for something uniquely you – a manner, a glance, a laugh. Our foolish love is a sign that we would be too daft to act rationally when offered a nicer vehicle for propagating our genes, and so justify our partner's belief that we will commit over time. Thus irrationality ('You drive me crazy', 'I can't help loving you', etc.) is the evolutionary key that opens the door to *true* love, thus contradicting the rational optimizer so beloved of the crude evolution brigade. Annoyingly, for Pinker, it is also the hallmark of *stupid* love. For the same irrational declarations

Can set off a warning light in the other component of courtship, smart shopping . . . Usually people do not want any suitor who wants them too badly too early, because it shows the suitor is desperate . . . The contradiction of courtship – flaunt your desire while playing hard to get – comes from the two parts of romantic love: setting a minimal standard for candidates in the mate market, and capriciously committing body and soul to one of them.[6]

Pinker's evolutionary story captures the dilemma of romantic love rather well. We must follow two contrasting love scripts. We need to do backstage tactical work so as not to appear needy, but we also need to lose our heads, to give in to 'the power of love'. I return to this theme later. This enriched evolutionary account is, I believe, wholly persuasive and utterly non-deterministic. That is to say it does nothing to explain why person *a* fell in love with person *b*, let alone whom they might fall in love with next.

The counterpoint to this account of irrational but universal love is to be found in the social constructionist story, nicely captured by La Rochefoucauld's oft-quoted observation that 'many people would not have fallen in love had they not heard of it'. For crude social constructionists, love is a modern invention governed by the interests of the powerful. One version of this is the feminist line that the ideology of love is a male invention. As feminist thinker Mary Evans argues, 'far from liberating women from patriarchal control of the pressures of arranged marriages, romantic love actually traps women in false expectations and psychologically crippling demands'.[7] In short, she claims, love is bad for women; in the case of Diana, Princess of Wales, love literally kills. Evans celebrates Jane Austen as the level-headed sceptic about love who detailed the 'idiocies of both men and women in love and never falters from her determination that only rational choice, and rational discourse, can provide an adequate basis for human relationships.' This, I would argue, is a rather literal interpretation of Austen. She may prefer understatement over gawdy emotional display, adult reflection over childish spontaneity, but Austen is clearly not making a simplistic preference for sense over sensibility. In *Pride and Prejudice*, Elizabeth Bennett's and Mr Darcy's eventual love for each other, given their original antipathy, could hardly be a more romantic story, however carefully and subtly expressed:

> Elizabeth, feeling all the more than common awkwardness and anxiety of his situation, now forced herself to speak; and immediately, though not very fluently, gave him to understand that her sentiments had undergone so material a change, since the period to which he alluded, as to make her receive with gratitude and pleasure his present assurances. The happiness which this reply produced was such as he had probably never felt before; and he expressed himself on the occasion as sensibly and as warmly as a man violently in love can be supposed to do. Had Elizabeth been able to encounter his eye, she might have seen how well the expression of heartfelt delight, diffused over his face, became him; but, though she could not look, she could listen, and he told her of feelings, which, in proving of what importance she was to him, made his affection every moment more valuable.[8]

But leaving that quibble to one side, Evans is wrong to assert that 'the accumulated evidence of the last centuries suggests that people in the West have suffered more in their personal lives from "love" than from any other single ideology', as though there was anything we could do about it even if it were true. The point here can only be that love is a bad way of organizing and justifying our relationships. Yes, many people claim (as La Rochefoucauld says) that they love because they've been taught to love the very idea. Sham declarations scripted by Hollywood and Mills & Boon (whether deliberate or self-deceiving) abound; but this can't mask the fact that our *capacity* for falling in love is universal and intransigent. We cannot force our way into feeling love for someone, nor can we force ourselves out.

A similar point comes across in anthropology. Charles Lindholm attributes the remarkable dearth of anthropological literature on love to Ralph Linton's influential textbook in the field (published in the 1920s), where he diagnoses that:

> The hero of the modern American movie is always a romantic lover, just as the hero of an old Arab epic is always an epileptic. A cynic may suspect that in an ordinary population the percentage of individuals with capacity for romantic love of the Hollywood type was about as large as that of persons able to throw genuine epileptic fits. However, given a little social encouragement, either one can be adequately imitated without the performer admitting even to himself that the performance is not genuine.[9]

We are often told how the Greeks had various words for love. How they distinguished between the altruism of *agape*, the mature understanding of *pragma*, the hard-won brotherly comradeship of *storge*, the playful affection of *ludus*. These forms of love were among the higher feelings for Plato and Aristotle. The lower orders of love included the obsessiveness of *mania* which was normally linked to the sexual passion of *eros*. Just how low these feelings were is captured in Seneca's belief that 'nothing is more depraved than to love one's wife as if she were a mistress'.

Only in modern times have we decided to merge these diverse strands into the quixotic ambition of 'true love'. Our lover must be erotically desirable and a friend for life. But this romantic version does nothing to disprove the universal quality of love, only the form it is allowed to take in different cultures. Seneca is not denying the existence of love, only describing its place in highly structured, kin-based societies where marriages are arranged (usually by the mature judgement of the elders) to further political and material ends. In these societies, love must be relegated to the illicit backstage and never used to justify decisions as important as marriage. The social constructionists may want to argue that the whole concept of love is a recent and contingent invention, but this theory is simply out of kilter with our knowledge of history. Listen to Sappho (To a Maiden) writing 2,500 years ago:

Peer of gods he seemeth to me, the blissful
Man who sits and gazes at thee before him,
Close beside thee sits, and in silence hears thee

Silverly speaking,

Laughing love's low laughter. Oh this, this only
Stirs the troubled heart in my breast to tremble!
For should I but see thee a little moment,

Straight is my voice hushed;

Yea, my tongue is broken, and through and through me
'Neath the flesh impalpable fire runs tingling;
Nothing see mine eyes, and a noise of roaring

Waves in my ear sounds;

Sweat runs down in rivers, a tremor seizes
All my limbs, and paler than grass in autumn,
Caught by pains of menacing death, I falter,

Lost in the love-trance

Charles Lindholm describes how, in ancient Greece, men would frequently fall in love with prostitutes. 'Though the channelling of sexuality away from marriage preserved the staid atmosphere of the family, it could have disastrous consequences when lust turned, as it sometimes did, into love'. Men occasionally sacrificed honour and wealth for the sake of a prostitute's favour, bringing disgrace and ruin on themselves. 'Although they, too, occasionally got enmeshed in wanton and destructive affairs, women did not have the same opportunities for passionate pursuits, and so instead lavished thwarted affections on their sons'. Love existed, of course, but it was never a good reason to justify any important decision, nor in fact an intelligible way of accounting for people's behaviour.

Things have changed dramatically since then. Courtly love, troubadours, lyric poetry, the novel, Romantic sensibility and the rise of freedom and self-expression have irrevocably changed the uses to which the discourse of love can be put. Only since these changes can pointing to love legitimately explain our behaviour. Edward VIII would have had a harder time justifying his abdication in order to marry Mrs Simpson in almost any other culture or period. Prince Charles's greatest crime was not to love Diana sufficiently, while his increasingly respectable relationship (she is now a divorcée) with Camilla Parker-Bowles is only justified by the widespread view that 'they really love each other'.

The social constructionists clearly have a point. There is plenty about the modern cult of love that makes people behave in ways that would have made no sense in previous times or in other cultures. In modern Western societies, kinship is no longer central to our economy and our politics. Nowadays, the ideal of true love is so constitutive of a good relationship, that to fall out of love is to declare a relationship doomed.[10]

While steering clear of the crude determinists, I side with the evolutionary claim (at least Pinker's version) that love is a universal feature of the human condition, while supporting the constructionist claim that accounting for, and legitimating, our behaviour by recourse to the language of love is a modern creed. Love is present in both unstructured and structured societies (past and present). It is mainstream in the former (who explicitly marry for love) and illicit in the latter (who, like Seneca, marry for anything but).

The fact that love is both universal and protean (thus very old and very new) is one way in which it defies easy description. As Francesco Alberoni observed, love escapes rational discourse and is either elevated to the ineffable through poetry or reduced to the comic through obscenity. The experience of falling in love (while often the source of extreme pain) is the purest form of happiness – true justification. Yet this happiness depends on an unstable see-saw between the need to feel free and the need to feel justified. It is no wonder then that in writing about love only poetry that can evoke (rather than explain) a dynamic process seems to do it justice. We feel justified *and* free when we experience true, requited love and this is why love is deeply unstable and maddening.

It is hard to find good relevant writing on love – writings by poets and novelists who show love obliquely through art capture the brilliance and the pain, the impossible choices and the complexities. The people who tell (philosophers, social scientists, moralists) are almost all beside the point or out of date. Love has posed dilemmas since the days of Eleanor of Aquitaine (c. 1122–1204), when love-talk became respectable, but only people writing in the last 20 or 30 years describe dilemmas that seem fresh. We don't talk any more of shivering sensibility, or repression, or troubadour chivalry. We talk of wanting too much and too little, significant others, and commit-ment-phobia. Love is of its time, like comedy.

The related ambivalence here is around universalism versus particular-ity. Cheap music tends to be potent (as Noel Coward put it) because the songs, like the clichés, speak of something we, and Sappho, would recog-nize. But our experience of love feels indescribable, unique, so much so that we look to poetry to give us new words and even then shrug those off with a desire to use words that have never before been spoken. Umberto Eco describes it nicely:

I think of the postmodern attitude as that of a man who loves a very cultivated woman and knows he cannot say to her, 'I love you madly', because he knows that she knows (and she knows that he knows) that these words have already been written by Barbara Cartland. He loves her in an age of lost innocence. [11]

The Paradox of Love

Love challenges our self-respect by always threatening to turn joy into humiliation. We may scorn the incurable romantics with their hearts on their sleeves, with their heads ever ready to flip over their heels, because helpless wallowing is degrading. But we can admire the same instincts if they inspire the grand passion of truly great lovers. Vulnerability from those who lack self-respect is pitiable; when it comes from Mr Darcy, it is the height of charm. Since true love at first sight *feels* no different from infatuation, we can only define what it *really* was in retrospect. We use words like 'lust' or 'infatuation' in most cases when either our love is unrequited or when we lose interest; we call it 'love at first sight' when the relationship continues to grow.

Whenever we fall in love, we 'take the plunge'. So to believe in love at first sight is just to believe in love – one is a subset of the other. In either case we commit to an image of our lover, and our future, which is uncertain and risks serious disappointment or pain. Love can look like a gamble. It may be that loving at first sight is a more reckless gamble than most, but from time to time even the most reckless gamble must pay off. But the other feature of romantic love is that it is beyond our control. We are helpless in the face of our lover and powerless to refuse their charms. So the term 'gamble' is misleading, since it implies that falling in love is a conscious, if unwise, decision. A romantic lover is not a reckless gambler, he or she is an addictive one. Better to think of an alcoholic who remembers how her first drink 'felt like coming home'. Dorothy Tennov coined the word *limerence* to distinguish a particular feeling associated with being in love as somewhere between infatuation, lust and obsession. She cited Stendhal's observation, that the

> most surprising thing of all about love is the first step, the violence of the change that takes place in [the] mind . . . A person in love is unremittingly and uninterruptedly occupied with the image of [the] beloved.[12]

There is no safe way to love someone: without taking a risk, we are not in love. And just as avoiding the possibility of humiliation means avoiding the possibility of applause, for the same reasons avoiding risk is avoiding love. *You can only love someone who has the power to hurt you*, and by the same token, you can only be loved by someone you have the power to hurt. In other words, we are simultaneously on the stage and in the audience – free, exposed, vulnerable actors on the stage *and* stonily, silent judges in the audience. This is the paradoxical relationship between feeling free and feeling justified.

Having the power to hurt the one you love simply means being an adequate audience for them – that unless you have the freedom to boo, the applause they need from you is not worth having. It would be utter humiliation to realize that the applause from one's lover was canned, craven or charitable. One need only imagine a stronger, freer audience laughing at one bowing to the canned applause. This is the essence of shame – true love is to crave the applause of the free audience, and to risk the booing. This is why Sartre comments that the lover 'wants to possess a freedom as freedom' – the infinite regress of paradox looms into view here since 'the lover demands a pledge, yet is irritated by the pledge. He wants to be loved by a freedom, but demands that this freedom as freedom should no longer be free'.[13] The paradox of love is the need to embrace what is forever receding and to withdraw from every embrace in return. Recede too far and you walk free of the relationship; embrace too much and you lose yourself – make yourself unfit to be a potent audience.

Head versus Heart

It is tricky business for us to be open enough to lose ourselves without being so open as to lose our self-respect. The need to fall in love from a position of strength is self-contradictory, requiring us to stand tall while remaining weak at the knees – a perfect illustration of the theme of this book. To be happy we need to feel justified (loved), but not at any price. We must be loved by someone whose love is hard to win.

The initial fascination of love at first sight (more than physical attraction) is tied to an insight that this new person could be a potent audience. The more potent, the more we yearn for approval, and yet the more we yearn for approval the more we risk becoming craven and unlovable. We know we should be unforced and natural, true to our selves, if we are to be worthy of love, and yet we adopt tactics. Authenticity demands that our heart should rule our head, or as the Enlightenment philosopher David Hume put it, 'reason should be the slave of the passions', but passion without reason is at best a childish fantasy. Indeed, the very idea is incoherent when we recall Goffman's claim that a self, whether independent or insipid, is 'a dramatic achievement'.[14] We are always performing appropriately to manage impressions, and so must adopt tactics. If, however, we are *merely* tactical, all head no heart, we are being equally incoherent. So the question is *How cautious to be?*

The safest tactic comes from being uncompromising and apparently indifferent as a default setting. For some, like Miss Havisham in Charles Dickens's *Great Expectations*, this is a reaction to failed love, for others it is a pre-emptive strike – they are never fooled and never disappointed if they follow Dorothy Parker's advice:

> By the time you swear you're his,
> Shivering and sighing,
> And he vows his passion is
> Infinite, undying –
> Lady make a note of this:
> One of you is lying.[15]

Knowing cynics may work so hard to forget that their air of control and detachment is a choice of one among many dramatic roles that it becomes their sole repertory. And this route, which while being the safest way to avoid humiliation, is the safest way (along with being craven) to avoid love too. As sociologist Ulrich Beck points out:

> Even cynicism sometimes fails to conceal that it is an embittered late variant of love. People raise the drawbridges of their longings because this seems the only, the best way of protecting themselves against unbearable pain.[16]

If this is too high a price to pay and we abandon cynicism as an option, we enter the risky business of balancing our tactical heads with our vulnerable hearts. Some of the tactics of approval come out strongly in meeting someone new whose likes you try too hard or, more rarely, not hard enough to match with your own. You watch a film together, and if you are interested in the person, you calibrate your reactions by an assessment of their own reactions and they in turn couch their language to echo yours to a reasonable degree. That it be *reasonable* is key. If you are not eager enough to please (too silent or too brazen), to establish common ground, you may risk being ignored entirely. If you are too eager, you run the same risk. You can take the risk of being unreasonable (of violently disagreeing with every view you hear, for example) as long as you are sufficiently sure of your own attractiveness already that you don't have to reach out. This then becomes an even better tactic, as long as you haven't miscalculated! One thing should be clear – this is not a matter of integrity, for to repeat Auden's line, 'sincerity is technique'. As I argued earlier, we are all micro-managing impressions others have of us (while barely conscious of the fact). Those truly indifferent to opinion could never be embarrassed by a revelation of their ignorance, cowardliness, laziness, lack of hygiene or other best concealed traits, and would have no problem being seen as craven or needy. Those people also run around the streets naked, claiming to be Napoleon.

We need love, but we disqualify ourselves from experiencing it by being over-eager or indifferent. The central claim of this book is that the pursuit of happiness is paradoxical in that the need to be free is an attempt to give up on justification, to render audiences impotent, and in the process it gives us the greatest chance of being applauded by our potent audiences. By being free, being ourselves enough not to chase love, we qualify as lovable. So our chances of experiencing true love, like feeling truly justified, come from expressing enough, but not too much, indifference to it. Our films and books are littered with advice against being seen to be trying too hard. Yeats said it best in his poem 'Never Give all the Heart':

> NEVER give all the heart, for love
> Will hardly seem worth thinking of
> To passionate women if it seem
> Certain, and they never dream
> That it fades out from kiss to kiss;
> For everything that's lovely is
> But a brief, dreamy, kind delight.
> O never give the heart outright,

For they, for all smooth lips can say,
Have given their hearts up to the play.
And who could play it well enough
If deaf and dumb and blind with love?
He that made this knows all the cost,
For he gave all his heart and lost.

We know 'the rules': always leave them wanting more, never call first after the first date, never use the word love, don't look too eager, be cool . . . And yet, when lightning strikes we break all these sensible rules in a desperate rush to lay our dreams beneath our lover's feet and beg our lover, as Yeats does in another poem, to tread softly. If this loss of control doesn't enter the story we will never persuade our lover, quite understandably (and well explained by Pinker), to believe us. As Bertrand Russell put it in *The Conquest of Happiness*, 'Of all forms of caution, caution in love is perhaps the most fatal to true happiness.'

Fireside Love

There is an alternative view of love that is neither so denigrated as tactical compromise nor so glamorous as the bewitchment of romantic love. This is the picture of love growing, as a joint project, over time. Robert Louis Stevenson offers this counterpoint to love at first sight:

> Marriage is one long conversation chequered by disputes, but in the intervals the whole material of life is turned over and over. The two persons more and more adapt their motions, one to suit the other, and in the process of time, without sound of trumpets, they conduct each other into new worlds of thought.

This is a conception of love neither as a helpless falling nor as a tactical withholding of true belief. It is about companionship, intimacy, contentment, a warm hearth and respite from the anarchy of longing for love. As when Marie in *When Harry Met Sally* turned to her new husband Jess and said 'Tell me I'll never have to be out there again.' This is more like *agape* and *pragma* than *eros* and *mania*. This fireside love-without-trumpets may seem a humble variant, but many would be pleased to have familiarity breeding contentment rather than contempt. Passionate love is inherently unstable, and we can only hope it turns to this glowing fireside version once the flames have died down. The alternative is to explode or to turn to ashes. The more we tire of the tumult, the anxiety or the solitude, the more this cosy love becomes an ideal.

The strength of fireside love, a joint sense of home, comes from the idea that we take on each other's shape. If successful we become so idiosyncratically twisted by thoughts and behaviour into the shape of our lover that someone new could never be as compatible. Forever in love, hand in glove. Yet there is danger in this version of love too. In fact, if this quiet love is true love, it is predicated on exactly the same paradoxical dangers as the sound of trumpets. When companionship becomes taken for granted then our true love has quietly turned stupid; we are gradually bowing before canned laughter. Adequate applause is what we need, and the calm contentment of Stevenson's ideal quickly becomes the restraining cage – the codes we must break. Adam Phillips describes the problem well:

> There is always the taken-for-granted relationship and the precarious relationship, the comforting routine and the exciting risk. The language won't let us mix them up. We have safety and danger, habit and passion, love and lust, attachment and desire, marriage and affairs. We are not mixed up enough. In other words we still have bodies and souls.[17]

While cosy, fireside love is as easily idealized as grand passion, it is a complacent caricature to see it as more stable than its tempestuous cousin. The movement that undermines fireside love may be more gradual than revolutionary, but cancer is just as lethal as a car crash. As Bertold Brecht once put it, 'the ordeals in the mountains lie behind us / ahead lie the ordeals in the plains'. When we look at the statistics, it is among the long-term, apparently stable, marriages that divorce rates are rising fastest.

The deception of fireside love is in its appeal – persuasive sometimes due to the family setting in which it often resides – to the notion of *unqualified* love. But for consenting adults there is no such thing as unqualified love. For love to survive it must be an active choice for each party. *Adult love is always contingent*. We make promises that hide this ugly truth. We say 'I'll love you always', 'better, worse, richer, poorer' and 'through thick and thin'. We try to conceal the transactional quality of our love, the contingency of it on high expectations, with the language of the truly unqualified love that we can express for our children. Yet, if we are honest, romantic adult love is nothing like parental love, however much we might pretend otherwise. Our children cannot be unfaithful to us. They can hate us but they can't betray us – especially in the first few years. Parental love of children is unqualified by an idea of who the child is and what expectations we may have of him or her. Adult love is constrained by both. The main challenge to this ideal of stable, enduring love comes from the urge to feel free. Erica Jong is Thoreau's reincarnation in her loathing for this cosy love:

And what about those . . . longings which marriage stifles? These longings to hit the open road from time to time, to discover whether you could still live alone inside your own head, whether you could manage to survive in a cabin in the woods without going mad; to discover, in short, whether you were still whole after so many years of being half of something . . . Five years of marriage had me . . . itchy for solitude.[18]

Loving Couples

Apparently, the most successful lonely hearts ad ever in *Private Eye* was from a woman who said she liked laughing in bed. The combination of laughter and sharing a bed is a powerful conveyor of intimacy. The best couples laugh by day and are good in bed by night. Good in bed does not simply mean great sex. Witness Julian Barnes's description from *The History of the World in Ten and a Half Chapters* (the half chapter being about love):

> Anyway . . . she's asleep, turned away from me on her side. The usual stratagems and repositionings have failed to induce narcosis in me, so I decide to settle myself against the soft zigzag of her body. As I move and start to nestle my shin against a calf whose muscles are loosened by sleep, she senses what I'm doing, and without waking reaches up with her left hand and pulls the hair off her shoulders on to the top of her head, leaving me the bare nape to nestle in. Each time she does this I feel a shudder of love at the exactness of this sleeping courtesy.

And laughing together is just as intimate. To laugh (more than speaking) is to take a big risk, and an offer to invite laughter in return. If you crack a joke with strangers, you are taking the risk of being rebuffed. If they laugh heartily, they've taken a step towards you. True friends laugh all the time, and usually don't have to say anything particularly funny to stimulate gales of mirth. *If you don't laugh with your lover, you don't love them* – either because you don't find them funny or because you don't trust them.

Laughing is letting go – you expose yourself as much as when you cry. A parallel is captured in Leonardo's *Treatise on Painting*:

> Between the expressions of laughter and weeping there is no difference in the motion of the features, either in the eyes, mouth or cheeks; only in the ruffling of the brows, which is added when weeping, but more elevated and extended when laughing.

The romantic ideal that identifies true love with good relationships is not only sought by young optimists who don't know any better. People, however experienced in love or burned by loss, still cherish this dream. Usually the young are overt, proud of their idealism, while the more seasoned campaigners, who feel they ought to know better, often nurture the flame in secret. Elizabeth Wurtzel, an expert in pain, can't help outing herself in *The Bitch Rules* as an incurable romantic:

> Most of us need the conventions of coupledom, family and stability to be happy, need to give of ourselves body and soul and heart and spirit to our own true love to know the selfish joy of selfishness.
>
> So do not despair of the miserable example of your own child-hood and choose not to have a family of your own. Do not be denied by fear. No matter how much shit was visited upon you when you were young – so much bad that it occasionally seems like the best you will ever manage to do is hate so much that it hurts – I still believe we all ought to take the chance, the huge and potentially devastating chance, that we will be rewarded by loving that much.

Of course, the vast majority of actual relationships fall wide of the mark, and I don't need to quote divorce statistics to convince you. Many very good relationships start in love, and then fade to something more pragmatic based around partnership. If we strictly adhere to the modern claim that a lack of love is the end of a relationship we would give up our erstwhile lover as easily as Duncan Grant gave up John Maynard Keynes. In a letter to James Strachey, Grant explained how Keynes's

> feelings towards people, their strength and fullness, their purity of substance, even his lack of moods make him to me a most lovable character. But I cannot any longer believe myself to be *in* love with a person who sometimes bores me, sometimes irritates me, & from whom I can live apart without being unhappy, however much I like to be with him.[19]

How many people in a relationship can claim never to be bored or irritated by their lover or never to be happy in their absence? To hope for love to last in a relationship is at best an outside bet. As the humourist Fran Lebowitz commented:

> People who get married because they're in love make a ridiculous mistake. It makes much more sense to marry your best friend. You *like* your best friend more than anyone you're ever going to be in love with. You don't choose your best friend because they have a cute nose, but that's all your doing when you get married; you're saying, 'I will spend the rest of my life with you because of your lower lip'.[20]

Many would defend arranged or pragmatic marriages on exactly this basis.

Relationships can continue perfectly successfully without love, as long as both sides are prepared to conceal this lack and invest in being part of a good couple. In an age where love is the overriding justification for a relationship, most people are forced to lie. Since it is the case that to say 'I no longer love you' is to say 'This relationship is over', it becomes very hard for people to admit they are hoping to rescue their lover, or waiting for him or her to change. Most people are busy lying (faking the epileptic fit) that they love the people they are with, and a smaller number are lying when they claim they don't love someone else when they do. The cruel fact is that we can work at a relationship, but we can't work at love any more than we can choose which dreams to have.

The ideals of enduring love abound in books and films, but, while much less public, the widespread quiet death of love in relationships is something we know equally well. The pain of getting to know someone can become sharply acute when they suddenly look ugly in your eyes. Alain de Botton quotes Baudelaire's prose poem about the woman a man is about to fall in love with, whom he takes to a glamorous café for dinner. After spotting, sympathetically, a poor family staring through the plate glass he is stunned to hear his vision, his fantasy partner look with disgust and ask him to tell the owner to shoo those people away.

Love can seem doomed, since we know that one day our new love will disappoint us in this way, or vice versa. As she peeks behind his onstage performance she will discover his love of *Who Wants to be a Millionaire?*, his implausibly large beer-mat collection, or friends that do him no credit. It is little comfort to hope that she is so good and loyal to the idea of him that nothing she could find out about him would disappoint her. If this were so he would be left with the gnawing worry that he could take her love for granted. If she loved him in such an unqualified way, that he could never let himself down, that it didn't matter who he was or what he did, her judgement would be too uncritical to give him any true justification. Her applause starts to sound like canned laughter and she ends up with feet of clay for failing to identify his own.

Relationships, but not love, work through what Goffman called the 'sweet guilt of conspirators'. A private ideology that binds couples together. Ask a question and they look to each other before answering, they tell you what 'we thought of the movie' and what 'we like to do on holiday'. They merge before your eyes as collective identity comes to the fore.

Couples in public have a clear-cut distinction between front-stage and backstage. The rooms they clear and present for visitors include the living-room and bathroom (and more recently the kitchen), but never the bedroom or the cupboard under the stairs. In conversation they steer away from taboo topics and allow each other to perform the stories they have heard three times already and beam with pride or suppress their irritation depending on how well they're getting along.

When the couple is alone, the front-stage and backstage *seem* to collapse. An argument can move around the house with no boundaries, no taboo rooms. But this joint sense of home is an illusion. The couple still separate front- from backstage, the difference being that for a couple in public you have someone to share your sense of boundaries; you articulate them to each other ('Let's hide the porn in the attic'). *Within* the couple the divide between public and private is rarely expressed but no less real – drinking from cartons, furtive letching, applying toilet paper or tampons are all done in silence. We are so committed to dishonesty that we would condemn the young Bertrand Russell for realizing while out cycling that he no longer loved his first wife, Alys, and going home to tell her immediately.

Tactics and compromise may do important backstage work, but they are ugly taboo machinery that must never be made visible. A relationship without true love could never survive telepathy? What better describes true love, yet is more inimical to it, than counting the number of times the phone rings before deciding to answer it, or having sex and candlelit dinners with someone you don't like to avoid looking sad and lonely? In the early stages of a relationship we are fully aware, if only through introspection, that the gliding swan we admire is, beneath the water, paddling furiously. It takes teamwork to keep these ugly tactics out of sight. Sometimes the energy we put into keeping the relationship going completely disguises the fact that the hot spark that started us out on the journey has gone completely cold. As Robert Graves has it in his poem 'Full Moon':

And now warm earth was Arctic sea,
Each breath came dagger keen;
Two bergs of glinting ice were we,
The broad moon sailed between;
There swam the mermaids, tailed and finned,
And Love went by upon the wind
As though it had not been.

Desire, Fidelity and the Search for Strange

There are two 'conditions of love' according to Freud. [21] The first is loving a person you can't have:

> In some cases this condition is so peremptory that a given woman can be ignored or even treated with contempt so long as she belongs to no other man, but instantly becomes the object of feelings of love as soon as she comes into a relationship . . . with another man.

Our desire for what we can't have is a reminder that the part of a person that is forever receding in a relationship is often the most compelling. Similarly, many people lose interest in partners after they have, to use the brutal phrase, 'had them', sexually and/or emotionally.

The second condition of love is wanting what is bad for us, or relatedly, being bored by virtue. 'This last element may vary . . . from the faint breath of scandal attaching to a married woman who is not averse to flirtation up to the openly polygamous way of life of a prostitute.' Freud attributes this to a need for feelings of jealousy to heighten passion. This I described in chapter Two as the 'search for strange'. Adam Phillips describes the difficulty:

If it is the forbidden that is exciting – if desire is fundamentally transgressive – then the monogamous are like the very rich. They have to find their poverty. They have to starve themselves enough. In other words they have to work, if only to keep what is always too available sufficiently illicit to be interesting. Unfortunately, it is easier to fake obstacles – to simulate the forbidden – than to simulate desire.[22]

A Rabbi in the guise of marriage counsellor will justify the monthly (menstrual) period of abstinence in a marriage just as a sensible way to keep erotic excitement going in a relationship and to preserve it from infidelities.

These are all symptoms of our search for an adequately free audience. If we turn lovers into nations, we want a combination of Brazil and Norway. Norway is the partner you'd be happy to introduce to your parents: kind-spirited, reliable, civilized, but a little bit dull. Brazil is the stuff of dreams and nightmares, the strung-out heroin addict who gives the best parties. Too much of one makes us desire the other.

I began this chapter by commenting on how people contrast love at first sight with lust at first sight. The problem with the distinction is that it civilizes love and abandons all the erotic baggage to lust. Love should lead to platonic harmony in this view. In chapter Two on freedom I touched on the ways in which the need to be free manifests itself in unruly desires and disruptive urges. The classic domain in which this occurs is in sexual desire and fantasy. Erica Jong's notion of the 'zipless fuck' echoed in Sharon Olds's poem 'Sex without Love':

How do they do it, the ones who make love
without love? Beautiful as dancers,
Gliding over each other like ice-skaters
over the ice, fingers hooked

inside each other's bodies, faces
red as steak, wine, wet as the
children at birth, whose mothers are going to
give them away. How do they come to the
come to the come to the God come to the
still waters, and not love
the one who came there with them, light
rising slowly as steam off their joined
skin? These are the true religious,
the purists, the pros, the ones who will not
accept a false Messiah, love the
priest instead of the God. They do not
mistake the lover for their own pleasure,
they are like great runners: they know they are alone
with the road surface, the cold, the wind,
the fit of their shoes, their over-all cardio
vascular health – just factors, like the partner
in the bed, and not the truth, which is the
single body alone in the universe
against its own best time.

Uncomplicated sex is a perennial fantasy. When people claimed to be baffled that someone as desirable as Hugh Grant had actually paid for sex, they missed the point. He didn't pay for sex with Desiree Washington, he paid for her to go away afterwards. And since sexual desire is cultivated by the search for strange (the hottest sex is illicit), it is a fundamental challenge to love enduring.

Sex and infidelity are the sharpest source of contest in relationships. Sex has a non-negotiable quality – infidelity – a brute force that gives the lie to our powers of persuasion and self-deception. We desire desire, while knowing we cannot desire what we have. Yet we must desire our loved one even though we have 'had' that person. We cannot manufacture that desire or protect against its departure. Rabbi Hugo Grin used to refer to the moment when love ends as 'You wake up one morning and no longer like his smell'. Phillips again:

> In our erotic life work does not work. This is its relief and its terror. It is no more possible to work at a relationship than it is to will an erection, or arrange to have a dream. In fact when you are working at it you know it has gone wrong, that something is already missing. In our erotic lives, in other words, trying is always trying too hard; we have to become lazy again about effort, because the good things only come when it stops – affection, curiosity, desire, unworrying attention . . . .[23]

When we look at the tension between freedom and justification in the realm of sexual relationships we can see that the desire for each generates a complementary fear. The need to feel free correlates with a fear of dependence, of clinginess (commitment-phobia), and the need to feel justified generates what Erica Jong called Fear of Flying (or what Erich Fromm bluntly calls Fear of Freedom). As Adam Phillips puts it in the melodramatic terms favoured by psychoanalysts:

> The compulsive monogamist is like the compulsive libertine. For both of them something is too extravagant. For both of them there is a catastrophe to be averted. Monogamists are terrorized by their promiscuous wishes, libertines by their dependence. It is all a question of which catastrophe one prefers.[24]

Not that one can choose between these poles as if it were as easy as getting in or out of a cab! Many couples work with a predefined, if implicit, view of what would constitute being unfaithful. Most would say that sex with someone else is a fundamental breach of trust, though 'open relationships' defy this generalization. Some would say unwholesome thoughts or fantasizing about other people are small acts of infidelity. But if they set the rules so tightly that their lover can't fantasize, then at best they turn lovers into liars, because they will anyway. Worse, if they succeed in policing these glimpses of alternative lives out of existence, they render their lovers impotent. Better for my lover to be tempted by someone else and resist. We need to make up our rules, but not in such a way as to close down our partner's search for strange. Doing that would be an attempt to turn them into craven fans with no alternative. The solution can only come from recognizing the Janus-faced character of lovers who by turns approach and recede. The search for intimacy brings them near and the search for strange sends them away. But if they never go searching, they can never bring anything new into the relationship; more importantly, unless they recede you can never be sure they are approaching by choice. That is why parting is such sweet sorrow.

Whichever barriers we erect, the discovery that your partner has been unfaithful makes it crucial to know when the betrayal began. After such a rupture everything that one once took for granted starts to look questionable. We need to know which memories to believe. We can no longer trust the one person who could tell when you were and were not right to trust them. We need to know when our true love turned stupid – when our potent audience went from laughing with, to laughing at us (though this is a better description of how the betrayed, not the betrayer, feels).

The mechanism for fixing a breach of trust has the same dynamic quality as maintaining love in the first place. When there's an emotional crash, like infidelity, or maybe a public insult, the only way out is a ridiculous seesaw that gets less and less dramatic until the instability fades from view (though it never truly vanishes into equilibrium). She betrays him. The initial crash is a big tilt down for the person offended. For him to rise she has to fall through an act of genuine contrition. If she, the offender, hasn't fallen convincingly enough then he will fall again, until he can force her to show enough remorse. If enough remorse is shown by her then he can start to rise. In the process, painful remorse brings the offender so far down that it's hard for her to climb back up again, even though he is now ready to forgive. She, the offender, can easily become the offendee in this case because her partner now looks to be profiting from the genuine pain she has shown, which in itself is offensive. Phillips once more:

> The most difficult task for every couple is to get the right amount of misunderstanding. Too little and you assume you know each other. Too much, and you begin to believe there must be someone else somewhere, who does understand you. We have affairs when we get our proportions wrong.[25]

Happiness in Love

Ulrich Beck picks out the paradoxical qualities of love. 'The new era which has fallen in love with love, so to speak, at the peak of its technical and rational prowess, is abandoning itself to perhaps the last kind of happiness that resists rational powers, evades the grasp of modern thinking . . .',[26] and, I would argue, as with love, as with friendship, as with all roads to happiness. We have invented the de-traditionalized dream of love and happiness in such a way as to make it impossible to grasp, which 'draws its immense appeal . . . from exactly this fact'.

As Adam Phillips puts in his highly charged book of aphorisms, *Monogamy*, from which I have quoted so liberally, 'there is nothing more scandalous than a happy marriage'. The reason for this, as for happy childhoods and happy workers, is that people need a formula. People hope, and buy books and therapy as though happiness comes from some secret ingredient: a holy grail or magic pill. Of course, the state of happiness is overt and transparent. It is scandalous because its secret is that there is no secret, and in describing it we are easily reduced to banalities.

Let us return to Steve Pinker's nagging thought that there's a 10 out of 10 just round the corner waiting to whisk you away. This is as much a fear as a fantasy. It is a fantasy in that this paragon promises to make you feel perfectly free and perfectly justified. Combining the search for strange, the pleasure of someone new, with the dream of perfect justification, of being completely understood. It is also a fear in that someone out there reflects that part of you, the potent audience, who would laugh at the compromise solution you have come up with, would show your current love to be a sham. People often don't want to be exposed to new opportunities in case they cast a poor light on their current condition.

The only answer to the challenge of someone new is to flip the paradox over and recognize that your chosen partner must themselves be ever-receding in some sense. If you love them they have the power to hurt you, and they become the someone out there in the world who can provide you with the Nietzschean sneer – in fact better than anyone else could since they know you so well – and so become the most compatible person. The main challenge to identity in a relationship is posed by the ideal of submission to something greater than ourselves, while being brave enough not to trap your partner. We need to be devoted and independent. This was well expressed by C. S. Lewis in his poignant memoir written after the death of his wife: 'The most precious gift that marriage gave me was this constant impact of something very close and intimate yet all the time unmistakably other, resistant . . .'.[27] As the American sociologist Robert Bellah identified:

> Love, then, creates a dilemma . . . In some ways, love is the quin-
> tessential expression of individuality and freedom. At the same
> time it offers intimacy, mutuality and sharing. In the ideal love
> relationship, these two aspects of love are perfectly joined – love is
> both absolutely free and completely shared.[28]

While this analysis is true to the paradoxical logic of love, it idealizes the situation and ignores the fact that absolute freedom and complete sharing can't happen at the same time. Failure on either front leads to clinginess (too much submission) or lack of commitment (too little), but the problem is you can't just average these two out. We cannot insure against these failures because they are in tension with each other; they are not poles on a continuum you can resolve by sitting in the middle. Like a baked Alaska, love must be hot and cold at the same time. The tepid middle – not too clingy, not too remote – has no content; there is no Goldilocks solution.

Much as it would be nice to believe in a happy medium, equilibrium, true love is always mutable and must revolve around both poles over time if it is to work. Better to turn from Bellah's sanitized version to the darker but deeper poetry of Pablo Neruda:

> I don't love you as if you were the salt-rose, topaz
> or arrow of carnations that propagate fire:
> I love you as certain dark things are loved,
> secretly, between the shadow and the soul.
>
> I love you as the plant that doesn't bloom and carries
> hidden within itself the light of those flowers,
> and thanks to your love, darkly in my body
> lives the dense fragrance that rises from the earth.
>
> I love you without knowing how, or when, or from where,
> I love you simply, without problems or pride:
> I love you in this way because I don't know any other way of
> loving
>
> but this, in which there is no I or you,
> so intimate that your hand upon my chest is my hand,
> so intimate that when I fall asleep it is your eyes that close.[29]

Love, Freedom and Justification

Much common-sense rhetoric tends to link freedom with short-term appetites and justification with long-term, hard-won gains. Freedom is the cheesecake to justification's waistline. But this tendency to polarize freedom as damaging and justification as healthy is an oversimplification. The expression of the urge to be free turns into the search for justification, and vice versa. An example of this paradoxical quality comes out in Barthes' notion of 'faithless benevolence':

> *Trick* – the encounter which takes place only once: more than cruising, less than love: an intensity, which passes without regret. Consequently, for me, Trick becomes the metaphor for many adventures which are not sexual; the encounter of a glance, a gaze and idea, an image, ephemeral and forceful association, which consents to dissolve so lightly, a faithless benevolence: a way of not getting stuck in desire, though without evading it; all in all, a kind of wisdom.[30]

The kind of wisdom in play here, it seems to me, is exactly how freedom turns into justification. When two equally strong people (i.e., equally indifferent, not needy) come to *recognize* each other, they achieve the height of intimacy. Some might say this faithless benevolence, like flirtatious intimacy, can't be love only because it is too strong and unstable to be enduring. But it is the very fact of its instability that guarantees its intensity. Adam Phillips points out how 'flirtation protects us from idolatry'. In the same way that having your cake is incompatible with eating it, we cannot desire what we have. The only remedy is for your lover to be perpetually vanishing. This is why they must be your potent audience – as soon as their love for you is unconditional (idolatrous), they become impotent.

We want too much from love, we want it to be sublime *and* enduring. Framed this way, love is as impossible as desire. For this reason love requires faithlessness, flirtation with the possibility of ending in order to endure. Zygmunt Bauman's pessimism about lovers who share 'an anxiety deeper still for being soaked through with the premonition of failure' is also love's salvation. The first stanza of Auden's 'Lullaby' captures this 'faithless benevolence' beautifully:

Lay your sleeping head my love
Human on my faithless arm
Time and fever burns away
Individual beauty from
Thoughtful children, and the grave
Proves the child ephemeral:
But in my arms till break of day
Let the living creature lie,
Mortal, guilty, but to me
The entirely beautiful.[31]

The possibility of loss – if nothing else then the idea that we are only together until 'death us do part' – is necessary for the abandon of shelter that is true love. It is the most final way in which the audience on whose applause we have come to depend becomes silent. The fact that 'love is soaked through with a premonition of failure', whether the terror that your lover will meet someone else or that their plane will crash on the way home from a business trip, encourages us to discount the future and be more reckless, to invest in the moment with more abandon. Often a couple's love is re-ignited when an affair comes to light and commitments are made anew. And it is commonplace to note, with Joni Mitchell, that 'You don't know what you've got 'til it's gone'.

For the literary theorist Jonathan Dollimore, the fundamental theme of the human condition is mutability – change and stasis intertwining, replacing loss with store and store with loss. Sir Philip Sidney declares 'Leave me, O Love, which reachest but to dust'. Dollimore points out how, in

> the poet-lover's desire: the beloved turns to dust, even or especially as she (or he) reaches for the poet, who in turn turns to dust in the self same process. That's to say, not only do we decay, but desire hastens the process of decay: desire itself (re)turns to dust; life, desire, are self-defeating aberrations: 'reachest but to dust': the embrace of love is itself a dynamic of self-dissolution.[32]

The faithlessness of love, the contingency that 'reachest but to dust' is the heart of its terrible power. Echoing Auden's faithless arm, the uncomplicated and genuine affection expressed in a kind but transient encounter discounts any conception of the future sufficiently to make the experience all the more pure. Habits and complacency can be lethal to its chances of survival. Better to worry that our lover will run off with someone else or that their plane will crash on the way home from a business trip. For relationships to last those in them must embrace the danger, and recognize that their terrors, their glimpses of the end, are part of what makes their relationship worth having. This vulnerability to the possibility of loss is of course exactly the anxiety that comes with falling in love in the first place. To remain in love we must continue to fall and expose ourselves to the possibility of our true love turning stupid, and we must in turn provide that sense of contingency to our lovers.

How do we know when we are actually in love? The philosopher Martha Nussbaum answers this question with the word *catalepsis*.[33] Certainty, she argues, comes not from reflection, not from the kind of intellectual scrutiny Plato recommended, but from the enormous jolt of suffering. When Marcel, in Proust's *Remembrance of Things Past*, after persuading himself that he doesn't love Albertine, is told that she has left him, he experiences a cataleptic 'blow to the heart' of great force. Pain is central for the stamp of catalepsis. Nussbaum takes this a step further. The love Marcel now sees is not so much revealed by the suffering of Albertine's departure: it is *constituted* by it. Love itself is created, she says, by love denied. Love pressed out of recognition by habit is not exactly love. Where habit or analysis take over, love falls away. Nussbaum argues that 'to try to grasp love intellectually is a way of *not* suffering, *not* loving – a practical rival, a stratagem of flight'. By having the intellectual distance even to ask the question 'Am I in love?' Marcel was in fact undermining the possibility of love.

Dollimore is very good on this unbinding power of love, the fact that true freedom, true faithlessness, leads to death or dissolution. But the counterpoint to this is love's capacity to bind, redeem and endure. This is where it takes on a moral quality, and returns as justification, because for love to be sustainable and more than just infatuation, or what Dorothy Tennov calls *limerence*, one must sustain a coherent version of oneself in the eyes of an enduring and potent audience. Faithlessness (freedom) may be the source of inspiration, but it is inherently unstable and detached. Faithfulness (justification) may be the source of stability and loyalty, but it is inherently submissive. So on the one side we have the fleeting intimacy, on the other the judging audience. They seem incompatible, but both are essential features of the happiness that can be brought by love. The paradox of love is that it is both unbinding and binding. To be brave enough to enjoy the faithlessness yet brave enough to be faithful, to submit, is the key. The fear of exposure stops us doing either very often.

In *David Copperfield*, we see the movement between freedom (unbinding) and justification (binding) played across three characters. David mediates between his love for James Steerforth and for Agnes. David's love for Steerforth resembles Barthes' 'faithless benevolence'. It is subversive, amoral (the thrilling feature of Steerforth is his insouciant, charismatic power), and rooted in private fantasies. Dickens portrays Steerforth as 'a handsome, well formed man dressed with a tasteful easy negligence'; he could always 'pass from one subject to another with a carelessness and lightness that were his own'.[34] Agnes, by contrast, is the moral arbiter, what Nussbaum calls the 'compassionate spectator'. She is the audience for whom Dickens needs to hold himself accountable, in the light of her potent gaze. In *As Good as it Gets*, Melvin (Jack Nicholson) declares his love for Carol (Helen Hunt) with 'You make me want to be a better person.' Agnes is this for David.

In *Copperfield* Dickens shows that the two separable axes of true love are, to misuse the terms, *queer* love and *straight* love (in all senses). Faithlessness and faithfulness – libertinism and monogamy. Nussbaum's subtle reading of *Copperfield* (her chapter is entitled 'Steerforth's Arm: Love and the Moral Point of View') picks out the contrasting gestures that represent the two axes between which David must travel. In Steerforth the emblematic picture where 'he lay in the moonlight, with his handsome face turned up, and his head reclining easily on his arm' invites comparison with Auden's 'Lullaby'. By contrast, Agnes's gesture is of a morally incorruptible finger pointing upward: 'that solemn hand upraised towards Heaven!'. David refers to Agnes as his good angel, while she (without David's assent) dubs Steerforth the 'bad angel'. But this crudely moralistic view is only partly persuasive to David. If Steerforth could have been bothered to defend himself against Agnes's character assassination, he might have contrasted himself as bliss, curiosity and laughter with Agnes sidelined as the dull, admonishing parent. This theme is central to my claim that happiness is a paradoxical movement between accountability and dreaming, or, as Richard Rorty entitled an autobiographical essay, between 'Trotsky and the Wild Orchids'.

Many shy away from the challenge to move between these two realms and choose the excitement and instability of the transient intimacy, or the 'zipless fuck' – swapping finger pointing for finger painting. Others ignore the excitement and take blind comfort in being needy or needed, replacing choice with unconditional commitment. Both routes are crippled by fear. Dickens wants us to be brave enough to recognize the power of Steerforth *and* Agnes – of mutability *and* loyalty. Nussbaum shows us that, for David, 'there is romance in his morality and morality in his romance'. She goes on to conclude that whereas both Steerforth and Agnes fail to be more than cyphers,

> David achieves a human completeness that they both fail to attain. His moral spectatorship and his love are, though in tension, all of a piece. His love is full of sympathy and loyalty, his sympathetic spectatorship full of loving susceptibility to the particular.[35]

And this, in truth, is a fitting comment on Dickens himself. An author who can enlist Nabokov's highest praise for his artistry and Orwell's admiration for his 'generous anger' has found a way to live bravely and completely, between bliss and pity – free while brave enough to seek justification, justified while brave enough to escape from comfort. In this sense, David Copperfield (and so Charles Dickens), who is *more* curious and idiosyncratic than Steerforth while *more* generous-spirited and wiser than Agnes, does indeed emerge as the hero of his own story. In writing this novel Dickens has shown us one way to be brave enough to live within the paradox of happiness rather than fearfully cling to one of its poles.

In love we must fall and somehow must manage to keep on falling if we want our love to endure. When Sir Isaac Newton first explained gravity he asked us to imagine throwing a stone out to sea. If you don't throw hard enough it will fall into the water; if you throw with the force of rocket-power it will fly off into space; somewhere in between the two the stone will go too fast to land and will keep falling around the earth in an orbit.

But this image, with its picture of equilibrium, is too comforting for the vicissitudes of true love. To imagine love like this is to imagine there is a happy medium. In a truly loving relationship, the gravitational pull of the body we try and orbit is variable: our lover approaches and recedes, and in particular is directly affected by how close we come or how far out we go. Your lover needs to orbit you too. As Larkin concluded:

> The difficult part of love
> Is being selfish enough,
> Is having the blind persistence
> To upset an existence
> Just for your own sake.
> What cheek it must take.
>
> And the unselfish side –
> How can you be satisfied,
> Putting someone else first
> So that you come off worst?
> My life is for me.
> As well ignore gravity.[36]

CHAPTER FIVE

Work

Joe: Gold makes the world go around.
Bobby: Some people say that 'love makes the world go around'.
Joe: They're right . . . love of *gold*!
From David Mamet's film *Heist*

Work has many parallels with our experience of love, and it is no coincidence that Freud identified these two spheres as the central parts of a happy life. We may have mixed feelings about work, but we can hardly deny its impact on our chances of happiness. Whether it is a calling, a vocation, a career, a job or just a paper-round, we can picture a continuum of work experience ranging from deep personal motivation on the one side and shading into pure instrumental misery on the other. One might loosely reinterpret these categories in a way that reflects the discussion of love in chapter Four with a calling seen as a truly loving relationship, a career as a pragmatic relationship, and a job as a failed relationship. The unemployed (whether lottery winners or destitute) are single.

But let's not press the comparison since love and work are more often sharply opposed. For many, love is pleasure and work is pain. In Genesis

Adam is punished for his sin with the words 'by the sweat of your brow shall you live'. In consequence, Mark Twain (with his eyebrow raised) exhorted us to be 'grateful to Adam, our benefactor. He cut us out of the "blessing" of idleness and won for us the "curse" of labor'. For toiling, slogging, 'stressed out' people plagued by that 'Monday morning feeling', the very concept of a 'work–life balance' is predicated on work being something we *have* to do in order to live at all, let alone love. Something we must contain if we are to stay 'balanced'.

Ronald Reagan once commented that 'Hard work never killed anyone, but I figure why take a chance?' In a similar but more serious spirit, sociologist Ray Pahl in his book *After Success* quotes a man in his forties working in engineering and maintenance:

> I believe that if I go any higher . . . I will be working for the Company twenty-four hours a day. Then I should be married to the company. I don't want to marry the Company. I want to stay married to my wife and family. That's it, basically in a nutshell. Which is why I've got no ambition left.[1]

The locution 'married to the job' is supposed to have an oxymoronic feel. That if your work is something like a relationship then you have got things badly wrong. People dream of escaping, of early retirement, of winning the lottery and sticking two fingers up at the boss. In reality, we routinely break promises to ourselves – 'I'll be out of here in twelve months' – and stay in the same rut for years, feeling as resentful as Larkin did:

> Why should I let the toad work
> Squat on my life?
> Can't I use my wit as a pitchfork
> And drive the brute off?

Six days of the week it soils
With its sickening poison –
Just for paying a few bills!
That's out of proportion.[2]

The 'curse of labour' is all around us. We know our daily grind well and, through newspaper headlines if not direct experience, of the fat cats and crooked accountants who exploit the laborious produce of their workers. We also know our own role, perhaps less well, as the *consumers* of the products of 'cursed labour' around the world. However much we like to avert our gaze, we get glimpses just by looking at the 'Made in . . .' labels on our clothing. The social psychologist Michael Billig sheds uncomfortable light on this fact of consumer culture, along with the unpalatable process through which we obscure it from daily view (with the unconscious skill of the fattest of cats):

> If my clothes and other possessions are to be *mine*, then my imagination needs to be habitually curtailed . . . I should not imagine those strange hands, which once touched my possessions. Indeed, my possessions would cease to feel mine – and I would cease to be my good consuming self – if I took seriously the dark, busy fingers, working in conditions of oppression far removed from my life-world. Those anonymous fingers, no matter how many hours they labour, will never be able to own the sorts of possessions that I take for granted.[3]

Of course, for those lucky enough to work in the rich West there is another side to this tarnished coin. For counterbalancing our complaints about having to work is the fact that it is simply so important to us. In *Memoirs from The House of the Dead* Dostoevsky comments that 'deprived of meaningful work, men and women lose their reason for existence; they go stark, raving mad'.[4] It is so core to our identity that it is usually the first thing we say when asked to describe ourselves. Without work it is hard to build a coherent narrative about our lives or to feel justified in others' eyes. The old saw about people dying soon after they have retired testifies to this view.

Work provides a context through which the questions that lie at the heart of this book, 'What do I want?' and 'How should I live?', are felt acutely. In the way we talk about work, whether we enjoy it, or are proud of what we do, whether it sounds interesting to others, whether we have power, fame, wealth or dignity, we mark out our sense of self-worth in ways much more significant than is easy to admit. However much I try to avoid it, if I meet a stranger at a party and hear she is a firefighter, a musician or a merchant banker, associations with those jobs inevitably colour my sense of her (and vice versa no doubt). It gives me a glimpse (a first impression, to be adjusted as I learn more) of what she is good at and what she cares about. And during that conversation, since we both know that these judgements are being made, the process of managing impressions, balancing the appearance of knowingness with the appearance of unself-conscious candour, is carefully played out. In these settings, for example, we implicitly convey but rarely spell out how much we earn.

Managing impressions in how we describe 'making a living' to others consumes much emotional energy since it is so key to our chances of a good reputation. Those with evidently glamorous jobs tend to be coyly modest to avoid the risk of sounding like a show-off. In contrast, when people are less certain of their status they usually produce justifying ('for my sins') language in an attempt at saving face. They often use euphemisms ('between jobs'), or elevated language ('vice-president safety pins'), or just bluff. Have you noticed how in surveys of public opinion, estate agents, politicians and journalists usually come bottom on trustworthiness and popularity? And in particular how, of the three, it is the estate agent, or realtor (doing the job lacking cocktail party glamour), who seems least willing to brag about these findings? A hack or minor politician, so sure of the cachet their roles actually command, will publicly chortle about their low scores in mock self-deprecation.

Power, fame, glamour and money can excite us, while an obvious commitment to higher ideals can inspire. We tend to be explicit about the latter, while being rather coy about the former. In fact, of all our motives to work, money is the most fraught. Quite apart from its instrumental value, it is a very literal measure of our worth to someone, and so a potential source of justification. The fact of money makes it hard to trust each other's and our own motives. While Danny Devito's character in Mamet's *Heist* exclaims 'Everybody loves money . . . that's why they call it *money*!', most of us are slower to admit that contempt for the filthy rich with their filthy lucre is often merely disguised envy. We hate money *because* we love it. Yet the simple fact that we are paid for our work makes it the antithesis of love and closer to prostitution.[5]

Money seriously distorts our ability to think clearly about why we work since there is something intrinsically demeaning about being paid for activity that is also important for other reasons. Psychologists call this the 'over-justification effect' and have found that people doing charitable work (i.e., for free) became much less happy when given the 'incentive' of money for the same tasks. The degrading presence of cash turns what was once a 'calling' into a badly paid job.[6] The presence of money, because of our desire for it, always weakens the possibility of trust in relationships. The obviousness of the financial incentive calls all of our other motives into question. I will return to this issue later.

So why do people work? An economist focusing on utility will talk of consumption, leisure and the income needed to afford both. Probably this description would suffice for many people on the planet and for most of our history. But for the recent, local and lucky few who have the leisure and wealth to think about happiness and read a book like this, we need more. We need to work in order to live, of course, but whatever we may do for that living forms a central part of our identity, without which (or a better alternative) we would feel somehow lessened. The indignity of being made unemployed is a reminder that even the hardest jobs are sources of more than money. Freud, in 'Civilization and its Discontents', observed that 'no other technique for the conduct of life attaches the individual so firmly to reality as laying emphasis on work; for his work at least gives him a secure place in a portion of reality, in the human community.' We are in love with love, while our feelings about work are more ambivalent; but it is at least a love/hate relationship.

In the context of my overall argument, it seems clear that work is a site through which we seek to feel truly justified. As I go on to outline below, work, in the rich West, is increasingly being described as a source of freedom and self-expression, while this very trend is bringing with it a crisis of justification.

The Rise of Work as Self-Expression

The idea that work needs to be more than merely the instrumental satisfaction of basic needs (e.g., food and shelter) can be traced back to the eighteenth century. Adam Smith's foundation stone for neo-liberal economics, *The Wealth of Nations* (completed in 1776 after twelve years of work), identified the capitalist engine of wealth creation while also pointing to its limitations in terms of its impact on human behaviour. In this seminal text he set up two contrasting insights, the first of which has shaped modern economics and much of industry. Smith saw that increased wealth creation would depend on increased specialization. His famous example of the pin factory makes the point:

One man draws out the wire, another straightens it, a third cuts it, a fourth points it, a fifth grinds it at the top for receiving a head;

to make the head requires two or three distinct operations; to put it on, is a peculiar business, to whiten the pins is another; it is even a trade in itself to put them into the paper . . . .[7]

With every step of the process split into components repeatedly undertaken by specialists, ten people could generate 48,000 pins a day, while each one would struggle to make 20 pins if left alone to create them from beginning to end.

Adam Smith's second, less celebrated, insight offers a prescient fore-shadowing of modern management theory. This was that too much specialization turned workers into unmotivated machines:

In the progress of the division of labour, the employment of the far greater part of those who live by labour . . . comes to be confined to a few very simple operations; frequently to one or two . . . The man whose whole life is spent in performing a few simple operations . . . generally becomes as stupid and ignorant as it is possible for a human creature to become.

Despite attempts to stem the rising tide of alienation (think of Marx and Engels urging 'workers of the world [to] unite, you have nothing to lose but your chains'),[8] Smith's second insight would be dwarfed by the impact of the first for more than a century. The dream of freedom through work (of creativity, self-expression and the departure from norms) was left for artists, intellectuals and entrepreneurs. For everyone else the sheer productivity that resulted from a division of labour (240 pins to one) had created so much wealth, and opportunity for more wealth, that alienation seemed (to their employers) to be a small price to pay.

Henry Ford and his Model T were the true inheritors of this development. Ford further intensified the division of labour by carefully designing his Highland Park factory to achieve an optimal flow of production. He mechanized the manufacturing process with assembly lines, and in the process replaced the traditional concept of a craft with the conveyor belt. As Ford put it, 'the idea is that a man must not be hurried in his work – he must have every second necessary but not a single unnecessary second'.[9] The 'scientific management' of Frederick Winslow Taylor (1856–1915) provided the intellectual grist to Ford's mill. Taylor saw workers as intrinsically self-interested, unskilled and lazy, and wanted to reshape human activity in the image of a clock. His, now notorious, time and motion studies were put in place to find the 'one best way' to organize any process and effectively reduce workers to unthinking cogs in a precisely designed machine.

But things began to change as management theory came up against the limits of control. It became increasingly clear that treating people like human beings actually made them more productive. During the 1920s and early 1930s, the Hawthorne Works in Chicago (part of Western Electric) was the site of a series of landmark human behaviour studies that examined how fatigue, monotony and supervision on an assembly line dramatically affected productivity. The results of those famous tests are referred to as the Hawthorne Effect, where almost any change to the workers' environment improved the quality of work.[10]

More to the point, the attempt to turn people into reliable clocks actually generated rebellion. As said earlier, too much routine makes people desire risk, and rules breed unruliness. Specialization leads to alienation leads to subversion. As a consequence of failed attempts to control workers, freedom has taken an increasingly powerful hold on their imaginations, and, in light of this, recent management theory has taken up the banner of individual self-expression and creativity. What has, in the last 30 years, begun to challenge the conveyor-belt version of progress is not any moral or political squeamishness, rather it is the law of diminishing returns that comes from running Adam Smith's second insight against the first.

New theories of motivation, flowering especially in the 1960s, introduced a more liberationist tone. The psychologist Abraham Maslow developed the notion of self-actualization and placed it at the top of a hierarchy of needs. The hierarchy has five levels of need: physiological, safety, belongingness and love, esteem and self-actualization (i.e., creative and aesthetic needs, the impulse to know and understand, to express uniqueness). According to Maslow, before a person can satisfy the need for self-actualization, he or she must satisfy other, lower motivations – hunger, safety, belonging. The management theorist Douglas McGregor was heavily influenced by this framework and came up with a distinction that has since become central to management literature, namely Theory X and Theory Y:

Theory X managers believe (like Taylor) that,
a) work is inherently distasteful to most people
b) most people are not ambitious, have little desire for responsibility, and prefer to be directed
c) most people have little capacity for creativity in solving organizational problems
d) motivation occurs only at the physiological and security levels
e) most people must be closely controlled and often coerced to achieve organizational objectives.

Theory Y managers believe that:
a) work is as natural as play if the conditions are favorable
b) self-control is often indispensable in achieving organizational goals
c) the capacity for creativity is spread throughout organizations
d) motivation occurs at affiliation, esteem, and self-actualization levels, not just security, physiological levels
e) people can be self-directed and creative at work if properly motivated.

Rhetorically at least, Theory Y has won. While there are many who have observed that people talk Y and practice X,[11] it is unacceptable to *talk* as though you believe Theory X these days. This liberationist rhetoric has enabled the thought that people often find their greatest experience of creativity and self-expression through their work. There is a tremendous sense of excitement and opportunity today as never before. Now it is everybody, not just artists, who can agree with the self-reliant Emerson that 'the reward of a thing well done, is to have done it'; or with Samuel Butler that 'every man's work . . . is always a portrait of himself'.

McGregor argued that after basic needs are met, the other 'egoistic' needs fall under two headings: *self-esteem* and *reputation*. This formulation strongly bears on the argument running throughout this book, that in order to be happy we need to feel free and to feel justified. But as I've also argued, too much of one becomes self-defeating if not redeemed by the other. Too much freedom, unredeemed by a sense of justification, leaves us disorientated and anxious. We are at a stage now where freedom in terms of our careers, as in other parts of culture, has been given its head and, relatedly, where the need for justification is less obviously being met. The best chronicler of this trend and its consequences is sociologist Richard Sennett, whose sophisticated and empirically grounded book *The Corrosion of Character* tackles the issues directly:

> Corporations break up or join together, jobs appear and disappear, as events lacking connections. Creative destruction, Schumpeter said, thinking about entrepreneurs, requires people to be at ease about not reckoning the consequences of change, or not knowing what comes next. Most people, though, are not at ease with change in this nonchalant, negligent way.[12]

An Era of Insecurity – Or The Crisis of Justification

Sennett's wonderful essay sets out a widely felt anxiety about the nature of work today. The book follows on from his 1972 classic, *The Hidden Injuries of Class*, in which he described the working life of Enrico, a second-generation immigrant working as a janitor. Enrico worked in an era when there was security and continuity. Work was linear and cumulative and amounted to a personal project through which one could articulate a social or moral identity – a sense of direction. Delayed gratification and long-term planning were rational strategies. Conveniently enough for his sequel, Sennett 'met' Enrico's son Rico on a plane journey and discovered that while Rico had the freedoms and financial success his father never had, he and his wife had to contend with emptiness and fragmentation. Rico lived an episodic existence that restarted every time he relocated. As a result he found it difficult to provide a continuing narrative, or set of organizing principles, through which he could express to his children the values of long-term commitment, trust and all the things that the flat and fast-moving new working structures fail to value.[13] The rhetoric and reality of modern careers emphasize liberation over continuity, freedom over justification.

Gurus now extol the virtues of 'portfolio careers' and threaten those who are not sufficiently nimble with obsolescence. The average number of employers in an American career is now ten, while the average even in Japan is six.[14] We no longer *have* jobs, we *do* jobs – in Charles Handy's language we are entrepreneurial 'fleas' flitting from one corporate 'elephant' to another. Yet, like it or loathe it, there is clearly no turning back to more stable times and authority. Sennett observed, while hearing Rico's complaints about his fragmented existence, that Rico 'in fact disliked the actual experience of rigid parental rule such as he suffered at Enrico's hands. He would not return to the linear time which ordered (his parents') existence.' And nor would you or I. As I described in chapter Two, once we get a glimpse of a life free of the structure that orders it, we can't help pressing against the barriers. As Sennett says, we can't go back to 'the deadening politics of seniority and time entitlements'. While that offered

> personal security and served a profound practical as well as a psychological need in modern capitalism (a self denying framework in which people accumulated a future worth salting away for), that achievement carried a high price . . . to continue that mind set today would be a recipe for self destruction in today's markets and flexible networks. The problem to confront is how to organise our life histories now, in a capitalism which disposes us to drift.[15]

The old days told you what to do, where you were, and the new days say you can be anything. Microsoft's slogan *Where do you want to go today?* is in this spirit. So along with the thrill, this freedom brings uncertainty, the threat of chaos, and, crucially for my purposes, a crisis of justification. The more we feel free, the more we need to assemble new, potent audiences in whose eyes we feel justified. We need a new structure and sense of purpose, which needs to be of our own making (not another return to 'the good old days'), and yet one we can believe in and trust.

It seems to me that the attempt to achieve a genuine sense of community in a working context, which allows us to express our personal *and* social identities, is central to our possibilities of happiness. I include personal identity here because unless our pursuit of justification is interchanged with our need to be free, to turn our backs on community and feel unique, then the justification we receive from such group membership thins out to nothing. Often when new recruits join a company there is a transition in their language from 'they' to 'we' that is necessary to becoming a part of the culture. Working in an organization, with a sense of common purpose and trust, needs to be turned into a collective experience if the company is to be effective and successful over time. Two ideas have arisen to meet this need, namely *leadership* and *teamwork*.

One might suppose that the need to construct a 'we' community implies a focus on teamwork and a de-emphasis on leadership. I want to explore these two concepts further in order to reverse that intuition. I will come to leadership in the following section; here I will briefly question the idea that teamwork offers a good solution to the crisis of justification. Surely, one might say, an answer to insecurity and an excess of freedom lies in the common purpose found in a high-performing team. Maybe so in some cases, but more often the opposite is the case. I believe many people experience teamwork as surprisingly unsatisfying, but have great difficulty in saying so.

Teamwork, I want to argue, through diffusing a sense of responsibility across team members, tends to work *against* providing a sense of justification. As I have said, in order to feel justified we need a potent audience in whose eyes we can feel accountable. Unfortunately, as Sennett argues, many teams are structured precisely so as to deprive us of such an audience:

> People still play power games in teams, but the emphasis on soft skills of communication, facilitation and mediation changes radically one aspect of power: authority disappears, authority of the sort which self-confidently proclaims, 'this is the right way!' or 'Obey me, because I know what I'm talking about!' The person with power does not justify command; the powerful only 'facilitate', enable others. Such *power without authority* disorients employees; they may still feel driven to justify themselves, but now there is no-one higher up who responds.[16]

To develop more concretely the disappearance of authority figures from teams, Sennett draws on work by the anthropologist Charles Darrah to show how in teams without *overt* audiences, the audience is, of course, the managers whom the new recruit is trying to impress; the art of feigning in teamwork is to behave as though one were addressing only other employees, as though the boss weren't really watching.[17]

The sociologist Gideon Kunda calls such teamwork 'deep acting', 'because it obliges individuals to manipulate their appearances and behaviour with others. "How interesting." "What I heard you saying is . . . ." "How could we do this better?" These are the actor's masks of cooperation.'[18] As Sennett concludes, 'in a turnstile world of work, the masks of cooperativeness are among the only possessions workers will carry with them from task to task, firm to firm – these windows of social skill whose "hypertext" is a winning smile.'[19] Goffman himself, after all, was the one to spot that 'since we all participate in teams (in front of audiences) we must all carry within ourselves something of the sweet guilt of conspirators'.[20] If teams are havens of guilty cooperation and power without responsibility, then it is to leaders we must look in search of our potent audiences. And it is from leaders that we must expect a sense of responsibility that enables them to function as such. Sennett laments the modern loss of the 'work-witness'.

> The employee labours in a vacuum . . . It might seem, logically, that this would free up the individual to contrive whatever meaning for work he or she wills. But, in fact, without a witness who responds, who challenges, who defends and is willing to take responsibility for the power he or she represents, the interpretative capacity of workers becomes paralysed . . . The lack of a witness diminishes the power of agency.'[21]

Follow the Leader

In his 'modernity knocking' classic *After Virtue*, the philosopher Alasdair Macintyre diagnoses the moral vacuum of our age as represented by the therapist, the rich aesthete and the manager. The manager is especially problematic, representing 'in his *character* the obliteration of the distinction between manipulative and non-manipulative social relations'.[22] According to Macintyre, bureaucratic managers are morally neutral, manipulate others and are manipulated by the systems they have created, looking for efficiencies on a purely rational basis in order to achieve the best return for shareholders. Whether or not Macintyre's pessimism is entirely warranted, the rise of the manager and management theory is undeniable. Before World War Two there were almost no graduate schools of business; there were schools of commerce. Now there are more than 600 business schools in the USA alone. The explosion in management coincides with the insight that too much control is self-defeating in a business setting.

Management literature these days prefers to talk of leaders rather than managers, or ideally leader/managers. Charismatic, 'situational' leaders, providing vision to win 'hearts and minds', who are simultaneously efficient performance managers using 'tumbledown management by objectives' and who organize and allocate resources to ensure results and accountability. The workplace is now a site for fun *and* profit, where people become *enriched* in every sense – fulfilled *and* wealthy.

The award-winning British television sitcom *The Office* is a *faux* fly-on-the-wall documentary about contemporary office life. It is routinely described, revealingly, by viewers as *painfully* funny, or almost *unbearable* to watch. The show is set in a bleakly unattractive paper supply office in Slough, west of London, where the central character, David Brent (regional manager), demonstrates particularly aptly some of the themes I am discussing. Here he is addressing his team:

Well, there's good news and bad news. The bad news is that Neil will be taking over both branches, and some of you will lose your jobs. Those of you who are kept on will have to relocate to Swindon, if you wanna stay. I know, gutting.

On a more positive note, the good news is, I've been promoted, so ... every cloud ...

You're still thinking about the bad news aren't you? [23]

This speech arises when the company, Wernham-Hogg, is faced with an office closure and has to choose between David in Slough and Neil in Swindon. The reason people describe *The Office* as 'painful' and 'unbearable' results from two features of the comedy of embarrassment. The first comes from the fact that financial gain and morality make uneasy bedfellows; the second, and more difficult, to accept is Auden's insight that 'sincerity is technique'. I'll address these in turn. On the first point, the language of mixed motives is nicely illustrated by David as he accepts a promotion from his boss (Jennifer) in return for agreeing to redundancies in his team:

Jennifer: I know that you're very loyal to your family here.
David: I'd be loyal to his [Neil's] family, it's one big family.
Jennifer: I'm just sensitive to the fact that you have strong, let's say emotional ties to your team.
David: Well, yeah, but there is the emotion as good in business syndrome, sure, notwithstanding the cruel to be kind scenarios.
Jennifer: I'm sorry David, you've lost me.
David: Well, you're not looking at the whole pie Jenny. Wernham-Hogg is one big pie, and if they've left me in charge of that one big pie, then I'll be in charge of the pie, and the people are the fruit.
Jennifer: I don't have time for the pie thing David.
David: Yeah, oh, well I'll take the job please.

What is particularly striking about Brent's language is his painful attempt to mix a high moral tone with self-interest. Parallels in management literature are not hard to find.[24] The first special issue in the 80-year history of the *Harvard Business Review* was devoted to the topic of leadership.[25] It is entitled 'Breakthrough Leadership, It's Personal', and opens with an editorial on 'Leadership's First Commandment: Know Thyself'. Breakthrough leadership is not just about jettisoning 'old habits' and embracing 'fresh solutions', we are told:

> It also means breaking through the interpersonal barriers that we all erect against genuine human contact. It's leadership that breaks through the cynicism that many people feel about their jobs and helps them find meaning and purpose in what they do.[26]

In a similar vein, management mega-guru Stephen Covey's bestselling *Principle-Centred Leadership* is a paean to this genre of enlightened self-interest. With chapter titles of the order of 'Primary Greatness', 'Seven Deadly Sins', 'Moral Compassing', 'Principle-Centred Power' and 'Thirty Methods of Influence' we can see many aspects of the battle to moralize the pursuit of wealth. The book has the following puff on the back from the editor of the *Harvard Business Review*:

> Covey provides an empowering philosophy for life that is also the best guarantee of success in business . . . A perfect blend of wisdom, compassion, and practical experience.

Things are little different in the UK. A recent book by leading management guru Charles Handy is entitled *The Hungry Spirit* and subtitled *Beyond Capitalism, A Quest for Purpose in the Modern World*. Two of his chapter titles reveal the tension inherent in contemporary management rhetoric particularly nicely. Chapter 5 is 'Proper Selfishness: Individualism can be

Responsible', and Chapter 7 'The Necessity of Others: "I" needs "we" to be "I"'. And, of course, we have David Brent's version:

> Trust, encouragement, reward, loyalty . . . satisfaction. That's what I'm . . . you know. Trust people and they'll be true to you. Treat them greatly, and they will show themselves to be great.

The language of management theory reflects the paradoxical quality of its task. In the words of the *Harvard Business Review* editor, that task is to create 'an empowering philosophy for life that is also the best guarantee of success in business'. In part this is no more than a consequence of the rhetorical victory of Theory Y, but in part it is also an attempt to sugar-coat the uglier economic realities brought on by the profit motive. As I argued earlier, the very presence of a financial motive generates widespread cynicism, which in turn creates the need for it to be offset with even more grandiose value-laden rhetoric. The implicit (though untested) assertion throughout is that goodness and profit go together. And this goes for real managers as much as for management theorists. Here is a perfect illustration taken from the Ford Motor Company website (November 2002). It is a message from the Chairman, William Clay Ford, great-grandson of Henry, and entitled 'Citizenship at the Core of our Rebuilding Efforts':

> Unfortunately, our efforts to strengthen our business economically will have an adverse effect on some employees and communities. We expect to reduce our workforce by 35,000 people worldwide . . . We will make every effort to make the changes as non-disruptive and mutually beneficial as possible. We realize that some of the things that must be done will be painful and will impact people's lives in difficult ways. But I sincerely believe that these actions will do the most good for the

most people in the long term. That philosophy – *doing the most good for the most people over time* – is what drives our efforts.[27] (emphasis added)

So how does a leader credibly do both jobs – 'strengthening the business' while 'doing the most good'? Much management literature cleaves to the idea that leaders are born not made (while offering advice on how to improve your leadership skills!). A leader, they offer, must be visionary, self-actualized, compassionate, strong, 'emotionally intelligent', hard-headed, moral, personable, extrovert. One way of creating this utopian mixture is to fuse these elements into the indefinable quality of *charisma*. The attractiveness of charisma as an explanation of leadership is that it makes the fluid and subtle interchange between the leader and the led on some level predictable, if mysterious. If charisma is an inherent trait, it simply does not require much additional explanation. A charismatic leader gets true followers in the same way that a flame gets a moth. He (it usually is a he) does not need to *do* anything to generate submission, submergence or followership. He just has to *be*. Charles de Gaulle captured the mystique:

> There can be no power without mystery. There must always be a 'something' which others cannot altogether fathom, which puzzles them, stirs them, and rivets their attention . . . Nothing more enhances authority than silence. It is the crowning virtue of the strong . . .[28]

Yet charisma has at least two failings as an account of leadership. The first is that a lot of non-charismatic leaders would rather this were not a ticket to play the leadership game – and they pay the gurus' fees! More important, though related, charisma is context-dependent. Management thinkers may say that leaders are born not made, yet they also recognize empirically that leaders are clearly dependent on the social context in which they operate in order to succeed. Churchill was a triumph in wartime and lost an election in the ensuing peace. Hitler is often on the list as a messianically charismatic leader; it goes without saying that – in a post-holocaust society – he would be less successful today.

But to say that context makes a difference does not go far enough. As I've argued throughout, there is a paradoxical and dynamic relationship between self and other. We want to be justified (trusted, applauded, loved) and we want to be free (unique self-expressive agents, irrespective of any justifying audience). The paradox is that in our pursuit of freedom we need to feel justified, and in our pursuit of justification we need to feel free. And this is as true of leaders and followers as anyone else. Once a power relationship becomes explicit we can see all the more vividly the dynamic interactions that come from the desire to be free and the desire to be justified. These are not static features of any context, they are endlessly negotiated between leader and follower. Much of management literature (like much of social science in general) turns this dynamic process into a static one. The approach tends either to freeze the leader (charismatic versus non-charismatic) or freeze the context (peace or war) in order to analyse it,[29] and in the process they emphasize one side of the dialectic while understating the other. If we are to understand how people pursue freedom and justification through their work, we need a more subtle understanding of how leaders and followers interact. Management theory likes to simplify the codes in play in a quest for control, but when the codes are followed too crudely and simplistically they backfire, as illustrated so beautifully by David Brent. It is in the moment of breakdown that we can see how nuanced and oblique a good performance needs to be.

In a recent review of the leadership literature, psychologist Alex Haslam identifies the limits of the static approach and offers something more dynamic,[30] by describing leaders as in an *active* relationship to the groups they lead, who are equally active in return. He quotes Adair's *Short Course on Leadership* to point out that the most important word in the leader's vocabulary is 'we', and that the least important is 'I'. To create a 'we' community, he argues, a leader must understand that the *personal* and *social* identity of employees becomes salient under differing conditions. More specifically, he argues that Theory X applies when there is a divergence between the identity (whether personal or social) of the worker and the identity that is dominant in the workplace. So, in the case of a union conflict with management, members of the union can only satisfy the needs of their own social identity by rejecting the values of the dominant social identity of the management. Under these conditions it actually makes sense to be a Theory X worker. Under conditions where the identities of leader and follower are more congruent, then Theory Y can start to look rational. Haslam's analysis is supported by a range of empirical data and leads him to conclude that

> Work *in general* is motivated in a manner consistent with neither Theory X nor Theory Y [nor the hybrid Theory Z]. Instead Theory Y assumptions will tend to apply when supervisor and worker share the same social identity, but Theory X assumptions will tend to apply when they don't.[31]

We can all agree that Theory Y makes for a better, happier environment for all concerned than Theory X. But the question is 'How to make it happen?' and whether either leader or follower can do anything to bring it about. This all goes to reinforce the importance *and* the difficulty of the leader's task in needing to inculcate trust. According to Haslam, leaders need to be 'entrepreneurs of identity':[32]

> Leadership, then, is a process of mutual influence . . . It is about the creation, coordination and control of a shared sense of 'us'. Within this relationship neither the individual nor the group is static. What 'us' means is negotiable, and so too is the contribution

that leaders and followers make to any particular definition of 'us-ness'.[33]

In the language of this book I take this to mean that in principle a leader has the power *and* the responsibility to satisfy our need to feel free and justified, to eschew 'ironism' and to be Sennett's 'work-witness' by creating 'a shared sense of us'. When personal identity is salient we express our need to be free, and when social identity is salient we express our need to feel justified. If these are congruent with a leader's identity, then s/he is in a position to help bring about an environment in which people can feel there is a culture they can identify with (social identity) and there are opportunities for growth or self-advancement (personal identity). That is to say, the effective leader stands as a potent audience to the follower in whose view the dynamic interaction described in chapters Two and Three can be played out. In turn, the followers provide the leader with exactly the same kind of audience. They circle around each other, actors on stage hoping for cheers and worrying about jeers, while simultaneously they are judges in the audience choosing when and whether to offer the sought-after applause.

Covey, Handy, Ford and Brent clearly have a point. If you want to lead, i.e., inculcate followership, then you had better be someone people trust. The point they tend to miss is that trustworthiness is in the eye of the beholder, and that it recedes from our grasp the harder we chase it. Of course, if a follower smells a rat, sees the leader acting hypocritically, then trust is lost. What is more difficult to accept is that a leader, shining with moral purpose and integrity, can lose the trust of an employee just as easily.[34] Think how easily a well-intentioned gesture can backfire, or how a perfectly reasonable person can make you want to wring his or her neck. Trust is bestowed – it cannot be willed into existence, or demanded.

The second, and deeper, form of embarrassment we feel watching *The Office* is not about double standards, self-delusion or mixed motives. It is more the unpalatable revelation of Macintyre's insight that manipulative and non-manipulative social relations are hard to distinguish. Without the dramatic skill to keep up a polished, convincing front, David Brent and his colleagues reveal their more crudely motivated backstage machinery. Through the incompetence of the characters we see how office life would look if we were less skilled as performers and impression managers.[35] The painful thought is that there is a streak of David Brent in us all. I should emphasize that this is not to say we are all venal, shallow people trying to con each other. Only that Auden's observation that 'sincerity is technique' is both true and painful. We don't despise Brent's motives really (that's the funny part), we are discomfited by his inability to *conceal* his failings – his stigmata (in Goffman's language). The difference between Brent and ourselves is not so much to do with sincerity as it is to do with technique. This exchange between Tim and his colleague Gareth, after the latter has been made team leader, makes the point acutely:

Tim: Team leader don't mean anything mate.
Gareth: Excuse me, it means I'm the leader of a team.
Tim: No it doesn't – it's a title someone's given you to get you to do something they don't want to do, for free. Right? It's like making a div kid at school milk monitor. No one respects it
Gareth: I think they do.
Tim: No they don't Gareth.
Gareth: Er, yes they do, because if people were rude to me then I used to give them their milk last, so it was warm.

So the paradoxical challenge for leaders today is to *inculcate* follower-ship in an age of freedom and self-determination; when reasons to trust or to follow are so easily challenged. They have to be skilled influencers, 'entrepreneurs of identity' who are able to break through the 'interpersonal barriers that we all erect against genuine human contact' and must rebut the cynical retort that 'this is all an act'. Their improbable task is to *manufacture* what Stephen Covey calls a *High Trust Culture*. The task is improbable because on the one hand leadership is about *will*, on the other it is less and less likely that we trust someone who is overtly trying to *make* us do so. The trick is to act so well, have a technique so good, that what Coleridge called 'the willing suspension of disbelief' seems warranted.

There is every reason to feel that the role of leader in modern organizations is more important to our chances of happiness, and equally our chances of misery, than ever before. Yet, as Sennett describes so well, power without authority turns managers into 'ironists'[36], who so riven by the awareness of the contingency of their own position lose their sense of responsibility. The net outcome being that the crude facts of life fall back on to the workers, while the manager has the freedom to keep spinning, with maximum mobility. In Sennett's words

> The manager who declares that we are all victims of time and place is perhaps the most cunning figure to appear in the pages of this book. He has mastered the account of wielding power without being held accountable; he has transcended that responsibility for himself, putting the ills of work back on the shoulders of those fellow 'victims' who happen to work for him.[37]

Or as David Brent has it, 'it's out of my hands – and even if it were in my hands, my hands are tied'.

Ultimately it is more important that leaders are trustworthy than that they are charismatic. But trust is earned not asserted, and more particularly trustworthiness, like sincerity, is in the eye of the beholder. Taking responsibility is now the most important thing a leader can do at a time when there is every option and temptation not to. The biggest outcome of the victory of Theory Y over Theory X is on the dimension of trust – high versus low respectively. Trust, I believe, is the central consideration in a working environment. Yet it is badly understood and full of the paradoxes that are central to this book. The next section attempts to shed some light on this elusive concept.

The Problem of Trust

There is no doubt, thanks to Theory Y, that managers and workers recognize the centrality of trust. Companies herald the importance of 'no blame cultures' and 'celebrating mistakes'. The *Harvard Business Review* tells us that leaders need to break through cynicism. Trust is not only nice, it's cheaper and simpler than the alternative. Distrust leads to Theory X, and means micro-management, error-checking, policing, security measures, legalistic wording, credentialism, backstabbing and panic when things don't work. As if in a direct riposte to Taylorism, the sociologist Richard Scase, in an article entitled 'Why We're So Clockwise', details exactly what happens when the dream of control, of *scientific management*, has been turned into reality:[38]

> This low-trust syndrome leads to excessive bureaucracy, a heavy reliance on rules and high operating costs because of the over-use of supervisors and line managers. Because workers are not to be trusted, they need detailed job descriptions. Because of detailed job descriptions, workers only do what is asked of them, no more, no less.

And sometimes they don't even do that. Our lack of trust is a pessimism towards others' motives, Theory X in action, which can become a self-fulfilling prophecy by denying people their chance to prove us wrong and prove themselves trustworthy. Scase again:

In fact, in a predominantly low trust culture, apparently enlightened changes in organisation design can produce quite opposite outcomes to those expected. Instead of positive, engaged leaders, the result can be despotic little Hitlers. Instead of committed, productive employees, cynical time-keepers.

In a Canute-like effort to reverse this tide, leader/managers devote time and effort to shoring up levels of trust. Articles feature in the literature with monotonous regularity, and values, visions, mission and 'balanced score-cards' are brandished with zeal. In the main, they fail. Badly! One survey reveals that, while employees approve of the values of their organization, they do not trust their leaders. Only 11 per cent of all workers in the UK strongly agreed with the statement, 'I trust and believe what the directors of my company say.' [39] In short, everyone knows that trust is vitally important and everyone knows that you can't trust anybody these days (some management literature calls this mix of 'realism' and 'idealism' Theory Z!).

The reason that organizations fail to inculcate trust is that they are risk-averse, and in their caution they undermine the conditions in which trust can flourish. The academic topic of trust is a favourite among rational choice and game theorists who invent scenarios that test out the strategic and tactical value of trusting. These prisoners', cooperators' and social dilemmas demonstrate that if trust is to be given rationally, then *homo economicus* has to do a lot of calculating! The short-term benefits of being a free rider have to be weighed against the costs of getting a bad reputation, which can lead to pre-emptive strikes against you and a spiral of tit-for-tat escalation.[40] These logical calculations are designed to show how to minimize risk. And one can see, in our language, how well the game metaphor describes these risks when we ask 'What's she playing at?', 'Whose side are you on?' and 'What's his game?'

But much of this debate is beside the point. In discussing the tactical and strategic benefits of trusting, we have moved to a different terrain. The game of trust always contains undecidable variables. Trust cannot be assessed rationally any more than love. Trust *entails* that we make ourselves vulnerable, and it is in play when we cannot be sure. It requires a leap of faith, not a rational calculation.[41] Game theorists and managers look for the *best* move, while in reality we choose to trust or distrust precisely when we cannot know the best move. There are many concepts that disguise themselves as trust, such as reliance, confidence, belief and prediction, all of which betray their colours by offering more certainty that we can have. People who talk about trust without risk, even with managed risk, are like the authors of the unwittingly tautological title 'Decision-making under Uncertainty'.[42] Trust is to risk as decisions are to uncertainty – the one exists *because of*, not despite, the other. When uncertainty vanishes, so does the need to decide; when risk disappears, so does the need to trust. Other deceptive phrases search for their certainty through necessity, as in 'I have no option but to trust you'. This forced reliance, like grabbing at twigs as you fall from the tree, is not trust either. Trust has to be an active choice among other options that, at the very least, contain the option of distrust. The suspension of disbelief must be willing.

The flawed *desire for certainty when we trust* works like its counterpart *desire for certainty when we love*. We either manipulate and conjure or we crave and beg; in either case we destroy the possibility of its emergence. The hard part for individuals and organizations alike is that to allow the possibility of trust is inevitably to allow the possibility of betrayal. And so there is stupid trust, just as much as there is stupid love. As mentioned earlier, the problem is that the stupid version feels just the same as the true version. We can only know in retrospect that we made a mistake. That real-ization, however much we 'celebrate mistakes' in a 'no blame culture', is humiliating, and the pain is not easily healed.

Trust can fail in two ways. Our first intuition about misplaced trust is where we doubt someone's motivation, but it is equally important to recognize that trust fails just as completely when we doubt a person's competence. Think of how the failure to trust the benevolent but ineffectual Education Secretary Estelle Morris led her to resign from the British Government, and compare this to the more conventional distrust of the technically skilled but rapacious US executives of Enron. In both cases our desire to count on them is misplaced – in one case because they can't do what they should, in the other because they won't. There are also degrees of trust. I might trust you to deliver a confidential document without reading it, but wouldn't trust you to look after my children for the weekend. In all degrees of trust there is an assessment being made of *both* motives and competence. Interestingly this is revealed in the management literature on the topic of delegation and 'situational leadership'. The art of delegation is really the art of making someone trustworthy by giving you confidence in their motivation and their competence. Managers are keen to be trusted and yet they often fail to grasp what it takes to bring it about. Scase again:

> The result is rigid organisational structures that kill initiative and innovation. If workers have ideas about how their jobs could be improved, they keep them to themselves. Because workers hold back their ideas, managers assume they have nothing to contribute and do not bother to consult them. The low-trust, disengaged culture perpetuates itself. No business school education, MBAs or otherwise, seems able to shift this basic culture[43]

The way people often think and talk about trust in organizations is by focusing, like game theorists, on its strategic and moral aspects. They rationalize that cooperation is necessary for any organization to function, and trust is essential to cooperation, to getting things done, and so being trustworthy 'makes sense'. This tactical approach brings a moral in tow, requiring that managers focus on honesty, sincerity, consistency, willingness to 'walk the talk'. But these traditional approaches are looking for more certainty than can be had. They offer a recipe: do these things and trust will follow.

I argue that rather than taking the strategic and moral view we should focus on an emotional and relational view. Trustworthiness requires a more interventionist stance toward others. Trust is not a safe bet, it is what the philosopher Annette Baier calls a *moral prejudice*. If we are brave enough to recognize in ourselves the need for justification, i.e., for others' approval, we quite naturally can see that we cannot count ourselves honest or sincere unless someone else says we are. Even when people understand that trust entails vulnerability, they tend to focus on how my vulnerability affects my trust in you, rather than how it affects your trust in me. We have no integrity unless that is a judgement we have elicited from others, and so trustworthiness is in the eye of the beholder.

Trust is a complex emotional attitude, not a belief. The philosopher Jessica Miller defines trust as 'a kind of optimism about how others will respond to one's trust in them'. She also points out how important it is to trust oneself as competent and benevolent. A lack of self-trust, she argues, paralyses moral reflection because pessimism 'about one's ability to follow through could undercut one's drive to engage such reflective capacities'. I take this to be saying that unless you are confident of expressing the freedom to be independent of others' judgements, and acting accordingly, you will be in no position to submit to their judgement when it matters. Our paradox persists. 'Thus, without self trust, confidence in one's ability to trust wisely or to survive betrayal by others can reduce one's tendency to trust', and if you don't trust you don't get trusted. To trust someone is to give them credit, to suspend disbelief willingly. It means closing your eyes and baring your cheek – without peeking. 'This is partly because trusting people involves seeing them as competent and benevolent, and gives rise to optimistic expectations of response to the trust placed in them.' Moreover, by trusting someone, I give that person certain moral opportunities, for cooperation, generosity, or beneficence, for example, which she might not otherwise have had. Thus, when I trust someone, I help her exercise moral agency.[44]

The problem with the individualized notion of integrity that saturates our moral discourse is that it fails to recognize that trust and trustworthiness depend on an orientation to someone else. It is a moral affirmation of the other and a recognition that they are an actor, and that they have the discretion to be your judge. Miller cites the experience of the sociologist Judith Rollins, whose *Between Women: Domestics and Their Employers* gives an excellent account of how trust that doesn't recognize the trusted as an agent and judge fails to inculcate trust in return. Rollins was regularly left alone in the homes she cleaned, which on the face of it looked as if she was trusted by them. But her descriptions of her invisibility to her employers caution us from imputing trust to them. As Miller says:

In one case, her employers left the house, locking her inside. In another, they turned the heat off when they left for the day. Rollins was so invisible to her employers that they frequently carried on deeply personal discussions while she was in the room. On one such occasion she actually stopped cleaning, took out her field notes, and wrote for several minutes without them noticing that their 'domestic' was doing anything unusual.

In organizations, as in the households that employed Judith Rollins, people are very good at relying on each other but very bad at trusting each other. As with love, you can only say you trust someone who has the power to hurt you. Annette Baier explains the vulnerability inherent in trusting by pointing out how we can rely on people without trusting them.

What is the difference between trusting others and merely relying on them? It seems to be reliance on their good will toward one, as distinct from their dependable habits . . . We all depend on one another's psychology in countless ways, but this is not yet to trust them. The trusting can be betrayed, or at least let down, and not just disappointed . . . Where one depends on another's good will, one is necessarily vulnerable to the limits of that good will. One leaves others an opportunity to harm one when one trusts . . .[45]

So how do people show their willingness to trust? By freeing themselves of the craven desire for certainty that comes from the attempt to control their audiences. They take risks and break rules and put a spotlight on themselves in the hope of hearing cheering rather than jeering. They break the conventions of security and the norms that mean never having to be vulnerable. They laugh aloud, express needs, disagree strongly, invite conflict, offer indiscretions (revealing self-discrediting motives) and in other ways expose themselves to the possibility of ridicule as described in chapter Two. Moreover, they expose themselves *on purpose*. And this is where technique comes in, because if you perform badly (use the wrong nickname, laugh too loud, gush) you risk looking like David Brent, and so the temptation to play safe is therefore very strong. But succumbing to that temptation removes the possibility of being trusted, just as it removes the possibility of looking like a fool. In return, our audiences (whether managers or managed) should be able to take responsibility for how to interpret our performance.

The audience has the power to humiliate and to justify, and so the responsibility that comes with that power must be made manifest. Leaders need to take responsibility for their power, must not be 'ironists', while followers need to commit to a project they cannot be sure will not betray them. The thing you can do to open up the possibility of being trusted is to do some trusting yourself and hope it will be returned. It has exactly the same dynamic as the search for intimacy that was discussed in chapter Two. People love witnessing idiosyncracy and unguarded expressions of emotion. It is a great compliment to give someone enough rope to hang you with.

Most of the time, in our attempt to play safe, we are using techniques to *disguise* our self-discrediting motives. My claim is that if we want to be trusted we should use techniques to *reveal* them. People never really know whether our polished performances are disguising contradictory beliefs. But I am not arguing for less polish – sincerity *is* technique. On the contrary, our revelations need to be *deliberate,* and it is for others to judge their trustworthiness. We and our organizations must agree with Samuel Johnson that 'it is better to be sometimes cheated than never to have trusted'. To be needed, we need to be needy, and so to be trustworthy we need to trust. Only by taking genuine emotional risks, acts of code-breaking freedom, do we have a chance of applause, of feeling truly justified. As usual, Richard Sennett has a pertinent observation: 'To restore trust in others is a reflexive act; it requires less fear of vulnerability in oneself.'

As I concluded in chapter Three, we cannot go straight for justification, but only look at it askew. However much we crave justification our only chance of experiencing it comes by taking the risks that override our craving for it. In organizations this responsibility lies both with the leader and the follower. What we would like to forget, but must not, is that sincerity is technique and that trustworthiness is in the eye of the beholder.

Happiness at Work

It will be no surprise to hear me claim that people work because it offers a way to feel free and a way to feel justified. Like love, work is a central mechanism through which we express these deep needs. You feel free by creatively solving problems, doing work that wouldn't (or better, couldn't) be done by anyone else, developing social and technical skills over time, shaping your judgement through the mature wisdom gained by your unique experiences. Similarly, our need for justification can be addressed at work through the feeling that we have responsibilities. At work we find potent witnesses on whom we depend for their good opinion and who in return depend on us. Managers choose how much we are valued by the organization through explicit mechanisms like performance and salary reviews. Colleagues and clients are audiences to whom it matters if we don't keep our promises, or simply don't show up.

The more the structure provided by work seems as optional as leisure – portfolio careers, more speed, flexibility, change – the more the role of the potent audience becomes undermined. More and more people see their own future and that of their current organization diverging. The consequence is that these audiences lose their potency, and commitment starts to look irrational. It is easy, especially on a bad day, to resist the idea that work colleagues or managers are potent audiences, or indeed that work can be a source of freedom and self-expression. In our more superior moments of aesthetic self-regard we can agree with Dorothy Parker that 'work is the province of cattle'. It can feel demeaning to acknowledge that a contractual relationship can contain so much emotional resonance. But we don't choose our audiences. Worse, that in an environment containing relationships as explicitly contingent on money and performance as work so obviously is, the likelihood of encountering true potent audiences is very high. The biggest clue that work matters is the acute discomfort we feel when our need for freedom or justification is thwarted. When we complain about our work it is usually couched in terms of these needs being frustrated. In our loss of freedom we talk about feeling trapped, bored, bossed about; in our loss of justification we talk of feeling humiliated, alienated, unappreciated, unrewarded. If work didn't matter on these levels, we wouldn't complain in these ways.

To repeat the theme of this book, the need to feel free and justified exists in a paradoxical relationship. This paradox moves our experience of work around a circle that is both virtuous and vicious. The motivation to be the star of the show at work may be linked to the desire to be free, to experience unique self-expression. Yet unless this stardom is recognized or applauded by our colleagues, subordinates or managers (potent audiences all), our stardom quickly looks eccentric. On the other hand, if we try too hard to impress, in direct pursuit of applause, we run the risk of receiving contempt if we don't assert our interest in the work itself, irrespective of the immediate judgements of others. As Sartre suggested, 'the attentive pupil who wishes to *be* attentive, his eyes riveted on the teacher, his ears open wide, so exhausts himself in playing the attentive role that he ends up no longer hearing anything'.[46]

What is compelling about work is that it is a powerful source of potent audiences. There are rules to make and break so we become alive and have opportunities to feel free and justified within that context. But, since there is always the utility dimension – money (tennis unpaid is leisure, tennis paid is work) – our relationship with our potent audience is artificial. If we think of other potent audiences like a lover ('You make me want to be a better person'), we try to conceal the transactional element of the relationship. In work, it is impossible to disguise fully enough that it is all contingent on economics; there is literally a contract in place. Yet, the reason that work is so addictive is that it provides a structure through which we can test out our self-expression and self-esteem. Many people seem unable to get this from leisure, like playing tennis with the net down, as it were. As Stendhal put it, 'one can create anything in solitude except character'.

The difference between love and work is that love tempts us to fear endings, while work tempts us to fear commitment. Obviously this is a generalization. There are cynics who fall in love and idealists who go to work (though the longer they are exposed to this unfamiliar terrain the less cynical or idealistic, respectively, they tend to become). But with true love, with cataleptic suffering being the proof it is real, we often avert our gaze and hope we have found something unqualified and permanent. In love we long for certainty, but because love dies if it becomes too easy, taken for granted, we need to be brave enough to release our lover so that s/he comes back to us by choice. Love must flirt with the possibility of ending in order to endure. In our world of work today, I sense the opposite problem. Work is so contingent (no more jobs for life) and instrumental (based on money and vagaries of the economy) that we are chary of committing ourselves and so become unable to trust. As soon as you see the work you are doing as a one-off project, a case study, a means to an end, you become less able to trust, and become less trustworthy in return. We need to trust that our potent audiences will not fail us, and we need to care about not failing them. This means we need to flirt with the possibility of enduring, of permanence. Many people do the opposite. By imagining that their work is temporary ('I'll be out of here in twelve months') they never commit, and so remove the possibility of feeling truly justified.

To exaggerate the point, I would say imagining that the work we do we will do forever is a necessary step to being happy. But this is impossible if the potent audiences – the managers, leaders and influential colleagues – are compromised by being untrustworthy. Once we sense the contingency of the structure, of how easily the potent audience can vanish, the structure starts to look like a bad joke, and only knowing cynicism is rational. If, on the other hand, we are persuaded that our potent audiences are committed to the project, and to us, the conditions of trust are in place. We can start to find a reason to get out of bed in the morning, to take a leap of faith and thus search for true justification and freedom.

Happiness at work is about reinvigorating commitment in an age of instant gratification. With love we need to be brave enough to break away. At work we need to be brave enough to commit.

CHAPTER SIX

Living with Paradox

It's official! On Monday, 6 January 2003, the BBC ran the following story under the headline 'The Formula for Happiness':

> Scientists say they have solved one of the greatest mysteries plaguing mankind – just what is the secret of happiness? The answer, apparently, is nothing as simple as true love, lots of money, or an exciting job. Instead, it can be neatly summarised in the following equation: Happiness = $P + (5xE) + (3xH)$.[1]

I wonder. In Will Ferguson's satirical novel *Happiness*™ we see a world derailed by the self-help book that actually works. It is called *What I Learned on the Mountain,* and according to its mysterious author Rajee Tupak Soiree it also describes the secret of happiness. The book will

> provide happiness to anyone who reads it. It will help people lose weight and stop smoking. It will cure gambling addiction, alcoholism, and drug dependency. It will help people achieve inner balance. It will show them how to release their left-brain intuitive

creative energy, find empowerment, seek solace, make money, enjoy life, and improve their sexual lives. Readers will become more confident, more self-reliant, more considerate, more connected, more at peace. It will also help them improve their posture and spelling, and it will give their lives meaning and purpose.[2]

The book sells in the tens of millions; its readers stop smoking, drinking, eating junk food, become fabulously rich and develop fantastic sexual prowess. With echoes of Aldous Huxley's *Brave New World*, disaster ensues. All the sin/guilt-industries (tobacco, alcohol, health, magazines, fashion), and then the economy as a whole, collapse along with everyone's sense of humour. Ferguson calls his book 'Apocalypse Nice', telling of a 'devastating plague of human happiness, an epidemic of warm fuzzy hugs'.

Given the dangers, we can only hope that the newly minted 'Formula for Happiness' won't be the last word on the subject. As Andi McDowell's character tells her therapist in *Sex, Lies and Videotape*:

Besides, being happy isn't all that great. My figure is always at its best when I'm depressed. The last time I was really happy I put on twenty-five pounds.

The Happiness Paradox book does not offer a prescription or a formula for how to live a happy life. It is based on the assumption that there is no such thing. Rather, I have tried to diagnose why happiness seems to be so elusive at a time of health, wealth and leisure.

To recap briefly. I believe that happiness comes from feeling truly justified: justified by the lights of *other people*, not by a non-human standard such as God, Truth or the *Guinness Book of World Records*. To be justified requires that we have the approval of others, which means being found to be acceptable, laudable in their eyes. Yet it is not enough to find an uncritical audience that will always accept you for who you are. To be truly justified we need to be applauded by an audience with the power to reject or humiliate us, and so getting true justification is risky business. It requires we express its opposite; namely the need to be free, to express ourselves. This pursuit of freedom throws us up on to a stage to perform in the light – the spotlight, searchlight, torchlight, limelight – and confront the possibility of ridicule. If we never freely get up on stage in front of a potent audience we will only experience the dark comforts of Nietzsche's 'corner dweller' or pretend to be justified by the sound of canned laughter. Yet the urge to be free is ultimately self-defeating if it becomes an end in itself (to be truly free, truly alone is to be mad or dead). But without it we will never climb on stage in the first place. Herein lies the paradox – to be truly justified, I need to be free.

My claim, that the attempt to be happy is a paradoxical aspiration, leads to a suggestion that we should accept and live with our paradoxical needs rather than attempt to overcome them. In this conclusion I explore the reasons why we struggle to live with paradox. It seems to me that there are at least three: one conceptual, one moral and one emotional. We find paradox respectively mystifying, ethically distasteful and anxiety inducing. I have touched on all three earlier, but here I address them directly.

The Conceptual Difficulty

One reason we find a paradoxical picture of ourselves difficult to accept is due to our very useful tendency to simplify. We like to categorize and classify, and are most comfortable seeing things in terms of logical alternatives. Up or down, in or out, black or white. We tend not to relish ambiguity, as when we see politicians routinely skewered on the horns of the challenge: 'Answer the question, *yes* or *no*!'. Yes *and* no just doesn't have the same force. We put our binary alternatives on a continuum, and then link them together with shades of grey. Recall the discussion of Aristotle's *Nichomachean Ethics*, where the virtues are seen as the middle way through contrasting poles – bravery, for example, sits between cowardice and recklessness. Our descriptive imagination, influenced by our perceptual field, looks for contrasts, polar opposites, and then for golden means between them.[3] Like Aristotle (and Goldilocks), we feel there is something fundamentally wise about a 'balanced' approach – not too hot, not too cold. We balance the needs of the parent with the needs of the child, we balance work and 'life', rights and responsibilities, short term and long term, etc. And there are clearly benefits that come from thinking this way. But when it comes to understanding *ourselves*, the ideal of 'inner balance' is no more than a comforting fantasy. That however much we like to divide our sense of ourselves between an inside and an outside view, there is no happy medium between freedom and justification.

The inside view is rooted in an individualistic picture of our identities as being fixed and separable from the opinions of others. In this pursuit of freedom we share Yeats's fantasy of shedding the outer layers,

> I made my song a coat
> Covered with embroideries
> Out of old mythologies
> From heel to throat;
> But the fools caught it,
> Wore it in the world's eyes
> As though they'd wrought it.
> Song, let them take it
> For there's more enterprise
> In walking naked.

Anyone who has studied the humanities or social sciences (*pace* the 'scientific' end of psychology) will take it for granted that we can never be truly naked, that we are irreducibly social beings. This is the closest thing to a consensus in these hotly contested fields of inquiry. But it is very hard to *feel* this conceptual argument intuitively. We may well recognize intellectually that the *social* permeates the *individual*, but it is hard to shake off the inside view that if you dig down from the social crust you get to the unique core. In fact, this desire to stand independently of the views of others, while hopeless, is precisely the need to be free that I argue we should celebrate.

Yeats, in his love poem 'He Wishes for the Cloths of Heaven', is equally good on the outside view, the countervailing desire to be justified:

> Had I the heavens' embroidered cloths,
> Enwrought with golden and silver light,
> The blue and the dim and the dark cloths
> Of night and light and the half-light,
> I would spread the cloths under your feet:
> But I, being poor, have only my dreams;
> I have spread my dreams under your feet;
> Tread softly because you tread on my dreams.

Crucially for my argument, even where we accept that both views have a role in our sense of ourselves, that we have *both* a personal identity (shedding our clothes) and a social identity (spreading them under your feet), we struggle to see how they are fluidly and dynamically interlinked. My claim is that if we fail to recognize that our sense of self is irreducibly social *and simultaneously* obsessed by uniqueness, we are likely to behave and think in ways that are inimical to our chances of happiness. We have to lose our sense of self before it re-emerges in a way that is fit for ambivalence.

I want to get away from the following picture, where X marks the 'happy' medium:

Freedom   ⟵   X   ⟶   Justification

(shedding)   (spreading)

And consider the better, if more difficult, image of ourselves as suggested by the well known duck–rabbit image.[4]

In this ambiguous picture viewers may see a duck, or a rabbit, but never both simultaneously. Moreover, the harder they stare at the duck, the more they become aware of the rabbit, and vice versa.[5] Finally, this picture requires an audience: if *you* are the duck–rabbit, *they* are always watching.

So it is not that bungee jumping is about freedom and charity work is about justification, where all we need is a fine balance. There is no such thing. On my account, freedom is the duck and justification the rabbit. They are subtle, interrelated ways we make sense of our personal projects, one always the figure to the other's ground. The very same behaviour (charity work or bungee jumping) may satisfy the one need or the other. A lot of this book has weakened this implication for the sake of exposition. To conclude as I have in previous chapters that in work we must flirt with *commitment* and in love we must flirt with *escape* is just to freeze the paradoxical move between these two. It is a lot easier to start making a distinction in crude terms, even if you have to reject your own examples once the argument is clear. Living with paradox is a struggle to let justification undermine and redeem freedom and vice versa. Arthur Miller once commented, rather pessimistically, that life

> is an endless, truly endless struggle. There's no time when we're going to arrive at a plateau where the whole thing gets sorted. It's a struggle in the way every plant has to find its own way to stand up straight. A lot of the time it's a failure. And yet it's not a failure if some enlightenment comes from it.

Yet even here we see the illusion of 'standing up straight'. On the contrary the 'crooked timber of humanity' (in Kant's phrase) is perpetually leaning too much or not enough. Justification and freedom are about contrasting stances toward what Freud called 'our relations to other men', facing toward and facing away, and vying with each other continually. We are *both* Nietzschean 'actors' freely announcing 'thus I willed it' as well as 'stones' justified by being part of other people's life stories and submitting to their judgement. And while, as Nietzsche put it, 'all action starts with forgetting',[6] when we step back to judge and reflect, no longer a free agent, the rest of the world comes crowding in.[7] In our lives we experience simultaneous, successive waves of freedom and justification alternating with each other.[8] We can't have the duck without the rabbit.

To help illustrate more vividly something of this interplay I'll draw on the iconic and controversial film *Thelma and Louise*. Variously referred to as a road movie, a lesbian fantasy, an irresponsible celebration of Hollywood violence, a feminist manifesto, an outlaws-on-the-run movie, an anti-men tract, *Thelma and Louise* caused intense public and academic debate at the time (1990) and since.[9] The *Boston Globe* ran two columns, notionally the male and female view, under the heading 'The Great Debate Over *Thelma and Louise*'. The man, John Robinson, thought of it as 'the last straw' and that 'male-bashing, once the sport of hairy women in denim jackets and combat boots, has flushed like toxic waste into the culture mainstream with the vengeance fantasy *Thelma and Louise*.' By contrast, in the other column, Diane White felt that 'there wasn't enough man-bashing . . . I wish they'd nailed that little weasel who ran off with all their money. And Thelma's toad-like yupster husband deserved more than just an emotional shock.'[10]

The film is about two women stuck in cramped, unkind lives and relationships who set off on a journey along which they get stronger and more alive by overcoming (male-induced) adversity. Men are the enemy in this film. An abusive husband, an attempted rapist (whom Louise shoots dead), an offensive truck driver, a seductive thief ('that little weasel') and the police. With each step their journey takes them further into the realms of hunted outlaws. The road ends at the lip of the Grand Canyon with a choice between certain capture by the army of armed police who've encircled them and certain death from driving on and into the Canyon. They drive on, and the film ends with the car frozen in its arc through the air and their hands held together and aloft.

The film is archetypally about freedom and escape, but it is a paean to freedom that turns inevitably on the theme of justification. Its absence and its rediscovery. By looking at their relationships with their partners and with each other I hope to show something of how these needs are expressed, thwarted and mutually reinforcing.

At the start Thelma is in thrall to her startlingly unpleasant husband, Darryl – a boorish cartoon cutout who provides much of the comic relief in the film. Thelma is constantly seeking his permission to live while he treats her with contempt – 'Is he your husband or your father?' asks Louise. On their journey Thelma experiments more recklessly with escape than Louise, she drinks harder and flirts with more abandon, but in the end she takes longer than her partner to cut the cord linking her to her past. When Louise announces she is heading for Mexico, Thelma holds back. She phones home. It is clear that a kind word from Darryl would end her adventure.[11]

Thelma's eventual turn toward freedom, and away from her potent audience, was crucially dependent on the impossibility of gaining applause worth having from him. Importantly, this is true in two senses. In one sense Thelma could never have had recognition or approval from Darryl ('the pig', as Louise calls him), and may as well have given up. In another she suddenly saw how little applause from him, even if it it were forthcoming, would now be worth, and in that moment rendered him impotent as a source of justification for her. Later when the police advise Darryl, on the next phone call, to 'be gentle' and 'sound like you really miss her' because 'women love that shit', it is so far too late that the newly liberated woman just has to hear the words 'Hello Thelma' to hang up. She is truly beyond reach; 'I don't know . . . something's crossed over in me and I can't go back. I mean, I just couldn't live . . .'.

Louise in turn loves the affectionate but commitment-phobic Jimmy. Their relationship exemplifies some of the themes in chapter Four. As she tells Thelma, Louise knows Jimmy loves her 'as long as I'm running in the other direction . . . Once he's caught you, he don't know what to do. So he runs away.' Now truly 'on the run', in her moment of extreme need (they have to get cash to fund their escape) Louise phones Jimmy and asks him for money. Jimmy hesitates before answering and snaps Louise out of her vulnerability. As a result of her withdrawal, the tables are turned in their relationship and he starts chasing Louise's affection. By the time he catches up with her, with the money she needs, he is ready to commit. He makes the marriage proposal Louise had long hoped for, and offers to go with them. But it is too late: Louise realizes that to involve Jimmy now would endanger him.

For both women turning away from their pasts is not simply about removing their need for justification in favour of freedom. They are freeing themselves (Thelma out of choice and Louise out of necessity) from old audiences in favour of a new one: each other (I'll come to the viewing audience later). And yet the justification they receive from each other is neither complete nor easily come by. There is plenty of conflict between them, with Louise frequently berating her ingenue partner. It is a staple of buddy movies that the buddies bicker, but in this film the ambivalence runs deeper. For example, after a shooting Thelma sees Louise in an agony of panic and fear and asks whether it was all her fault; Louise just tells her to shut up. And when Louise nearly crumbles at some kind words from Hal, the sympathetic cop, 'Louise, I'll do anything. I know what's makin' you run. I know what happened to you in Texas', it is Thelma who steps in and hangs up the phone. And at the height of their solidarity, Thelma takes the emotional risk of asking Louise about her rape, but her invitation to be closer is rejected. These tensions go beyond comic effect and describe well how we struggle over intimacy. How we approach and how we flee. The women alternate in strength, they cannot take each other for granted and so are sometimes potent audiences for each other. On separate occasions both characters comment that 'we get what we settle for' and by more bad luck than judgement gradually decide never to 'settle' again, except with each other.

At the end of watching the film I was struck by the fact that people in the audience either cheered or cried. The ending was both triumphant and tragic. This dual reaction gives another insight into how one duck–rabbit moment can simultaneously have different interpretations. The first was as the culmination of a *private* journey; as two women's wonderful indulgence in the fantasy of making themselves anew; taking increasingly anarchic steps and breaking loose from society; a closing scene that is a celebration of the final act of self-creation – ecstatic self-destruction.[12] The second reading was as a *public*, or political, journey, where the film acts as a polemic declaiming the pervasiveness of male violence and oppression, where the final scene is a doomed recognition of the appalling consequences of trying to undermine a male-dominated world (they were never going to drink margaritas on a Mexican beach). Like the duck–rabbit, they are simultaneous yet quite separate readings because the call of the wild that inspires the first reading is unencumbered by the morality play of the second while depending on it for a backdrop. The second reading, about the need for justification being frustrated, itself generates their urge to be free. One would not exist without the other. But this is too neat a distinction between a freedom reading versus a justification reading. *Within* the triumphant reading we have seen the interplay at work, the rediscovery of freedom and justification together, as is definitive of any happy ending.[13]

Thelma: Now what?
Louise: We're not giving up, Thelma.
Thelma: Then let's not get caught.
Louise: What are you talkin' about?
Thelma *(indicating the Grand Canyon)*: Go.
Louise: Go?
(Thelma is smiling at her)
Thelma: Go.
(They are still looking at each other really hard)
Thelma: You're a good friend.
Louise: You, too, sweetie, the best.
(They smile broadly, hug each other, hold hands, and drive over the edge)

At that brief moment they achieve a combination of freedom and justification (in each other's and our eyes) that seems genuinely blended and as short-lived as all such fusions must be. In Yeats's words they were 'blesséd and could bless'.

A moment's thought, or a good film, reveals how much more complex we are than we'd like to appear to be. Yet we struggle to live as though this is true. Instead we oversimplify and cling to our old habits. We overstate or deny the importance of our needs, and dream up more certainty about ourselves, others and ideas than is available. We use language that polarizes the options and then idealizes and idolizes the happy medium, as we can see in phrases like 'everything in moderation'. In so doing we make the fluid static.

We live as though we have a fixed self and a fixed relationship to other people. We routinely describe as 'the real me' what is little more than a collection of habits.[14] The consequence of simplifying in this way is that we close off an appreciation of how our needs compete, how we are, as psychoanalysts put it, 'divided against ourselves'. We may recognize contradictions – we want to both smoke and avoid lung cancer, to have our cake and eat it. We've heard of cognitive dissonance, but we take too much comfort from polar opposites with a fantasy middle ground. We know wisdom runs against temptation, but we don't see how these are expressions of needs that actually depend on each other. We have a genuine intellectual difficulty grasping how our need to be free is deeply tangled up with our need to be justified. As the social psychologist Steve Reicher argues, 'we should see social life as a constant movement from openness to closure and back rather than elevating one to the extent that it obscures the other'.

The Moral Difficulty

If we struggle to accept the conceptual picture of ourselves as a duck–rabbit, we have even more difficulty with the moral implications of this analysis. Freedom has nothing to do with morality, while justification represents all the morality we can have. The fact that the pursuit of freedom is amoral but laudable is troubling enough (as it is for Rousseau and Taylor, let alone modernity's knockers). In his book on Houdini, Adam

Phillips comments that 'we often never feel so alive as when we escape'. Yet true escape is death.

The additional and more controversial claim that justification is all the morality we can aim for runs against a stubborn yearning for an ultimate judge. Along with the *conceptual* fiction of the happy medium between self and other, we still live with the *moral* fiction of God and Godlike substitutes.

Even 'non-believers' are inclined to talk about something 'out there' or 'in us all' that guides our moral sense, and struggle to accept Rorty's recommendation that 'if we can rely on each other, we need not rely on anything else'. As he goes on to say, 'we should see what happens if we (in Sartre's phrase) "attempt to draw the full conclusions from a consistently atheist position"'.[15] Believers in God's-eye points of view will of course demur, insisting that there are other, more reliable forms of judgement. They will say that without moral absolutes anything goes, and that since anything patently does not go, we must have an 'innate' sense of right and wrong. I disagree. On my account our conscience is not a machine for cranking out decontextualized judgements about good and evil. It is populated by our audiences, past and present. The consequence of this claim is that 'sincerity is technique', as is trustworthiness, generosity, goodness, decency, integrity, etc., because there is no one or thing that knows what we are *really* thinking. What is so hard to live with, in this de-divinized account, is that without a reliable audience we are left with unreliable ones; so we need to perform with skill to achieve their good opinion. We don't want sincerity to be technique. We want to give and receive Polonius's advice to his son Laertes:

> This above all: to thine own self be true,
> And it must follow, as the night the day,
> Thou canst not then be false to any man.[16]

But this is false hope; a hook in the sky. The very idea of 'what we are really thinking' independent of an audience is incoherent. To quote Steve Reicher again:

> To achieve pride, to avoid shame or moral blame, is not something we do in isolation, but rather occurs in the context of the actual or imagined gaze of others who applaud or accuse us. Thus, to act in order to achieve pride, to avoid shame or moral blame is not simply a matter of ends. It requires us to have some understanding of how others stand towards us and how our various courses of action might impinge upon their evaluations.[17]

We need to live with a painful reworking of Rorty's formulation; something like 'whether we can rely on each other or not, we cannot rely on anything else'. Because we cannot receive justification from non-human goals, moral reflection has come down to earth – has been *privatized*. Unless we can accept this claim, then the idea of justification from audiences that runs through this book will remain opaque. We will believe that justification is available from non-human goals. My claim is that our morality has not only become privatized, as a consequence it has become *interventionist*. 'Never follow a multitude to do evil' may be a convincing moral injunction, but it elides the fact that we are always left choosing between multitudes. 'Live and let live' or 'Honesty is the best policy' will no longer do as responsible codes when there are no sky-hooks on which to hang our principles. An example of this comes at the end of Thomas Hardy's novel *Tess of the D'Urbervilles*. It is the night before Tess's likely death, and her lover, Angel Clare, is trying to soothe her fears. Angel is a confirmed atheist, but Tess effectively makes him choose between kindness to her and fidelity to his principles:

Tell me now, Angel, do you think we shall meet again after we are dead? I want to know.

He kissed her to avoid a reply at such a time.

O Angel – I fear that means no!' she said, with a suppressed sob. 'And I wanted so to see you again – so much, so much! What – not even you and I, Angel, who love each other so well?'

Like a greater than himself, to the critical question at the critical time he did not answer: and they were again silent.[18]

Angel, in thinking he has chosen between Tess and something bigger, has merely chosen between her and someone else (whoever in his audience he could not face after having degraded his atheistic purity). The moral problem in living with paradox comes from the belief that we can be or find 'a greater than ourselves', when all we can have is an 'other than ourselves'. Take the outlaw status of Thelma and Louise. They have killed a man, and committed a number of other crimes along the way, including robbing a convenience store. 'Besides, what do we say about the robbery?' asks Louise. 'No excuse for that. No such thing as justifiable robbery.'

But of course there is. The robbery may not have been justified in the eyes of the law, but it was justified to Louise and more importantly for the logic of the movie, justified for a sympathetic audience. As we see on the in-store video footage of the crime, Thelma robs with great grace and charm, and has her husband and the police who view the tape shaking their heads in disbelief. No pushover she. Whether or not their reaction shades into grudging admiration is less relevant than it might have been, since the audience that now matters most to Thelma most is Louise, not Darryl or the police. After sounding briefly scandalized by the robbery, Louise starts to enjoy the story, asking Thelma: 'Do you think you've found your calling?' Thelma's response is 'Maybe. Maybe. The call of the wild!' Her amoral act of freedom has generated genuine moral approbation.

The audience watching is invited to judge Thelma as morally in the right; helped along by the sight of flat-footed men dumbfounded by her audacity. Neither the Ten Commandments nor the law are available to help us make this judgement. As Rorty puts it, the only thing that can justify a belief is another belief, such as believing in this case that the law is an ass (or 'tricky shit' as Thelma puts it). But in this controversial film there is no *guarantee* that we will feel this way. No guarantee that, like John Robinson of the *Boston Globe*, we won't see this film as 'the last straw'. Which brings me to the third problem.

The Emotional Difficulty

Besides the conceptual and moral difficulties in attempting to live with paradox, the biggest remaining impediment is emotional; namely anxiety.[19] We are anxious about needing too much and too little from others.

As I discussed in an earlier chapter, many children learn that to expect love or approbation is just to ask for humiliation, and so they teach themselves never to ask for it again. They invest in non-human goals ('the stopwatch doesn't care about your ego'), pretend other people don't matter, but secretly hope the world will one day recognize how amazing they really are, as if to make up for unrequited love in one grand happy ending. As Garrison Keillor says of his tendency to bat compliments away:

> Actually, I am starved for a good word, but after the long drought of my youth, no word is quite good enough. 'Good' isn't enough. Under this thin veneer of modesty lies a monster of greed. I drive away faint praise, beating my little chest, waiting to be named Sun-God, King of America, Idol of Millions, Bringer of Fire, The Great Haji, Thun-Dar the Boy Giant. I don't want to say, 'Thanks, glad you liked it.'[20]

It is remarkable how easily people deny their ambivalent relationship to other people. A focus on the freedom pole enables one to imagine oneself above the fray. It is extraordinarily impressive and ridiculous when people persuade themselves that, unlike sticks and stones, 'words can never hurt me'. 'I don't need anyone' should sound completely crazy, but it is routinely said or implied. It legitimates an ironic stance toward others, taking off my Yeatsian coat, in which I can see through their judgements against me as contingent and unworthy of reply. Inspiring as this is, it is an inspiring illusion, an expression of what the literary theorist Harold Bloom calls the 'anxiety of influence'. For Bloom the 'strong poet' needs to have created something that no one has done before or even foreshadowed, and in the process kill off their father figures – the giants' shoulders on which Newton was willing to admit he stood.

It is Sartrean 'bad faith' to say 'I flee from myself, I escape myself, I leave my tattered garment in the hands of the fault finder'.[21] We convince ourselves we are choosing to 'follow our hearts' over 'mere opinion'. The second collection of autobiographical stories by the famously icono-clastic physicist Richard Feynman is entitled *What Do You Care What Other People Think?*. The phrase is uncannily self-referential and leaves us stranded between anxieties – full, as it is, both of judgement and injunctions not to take judgements seriously. Feynman used this line to persuade his future wife, Arlene, to free herself of conventional mores. He would not have expected her to reply 'What do I care that you don't think I should care what other people think'. To cling to a non-human goal (like 'the real me' or 'the Truth') feels like a safe option, but is, at its limit, only an expression of anxiety.

On the other hand it is equally crazy and utopian to promise or demand undying love or trust or good opinion. To feel we are at the mercy of others' judgement with no remainder. What of self-respect? In the pursuit of *guaranteed* justification we risk sounding like a love letter that the comedian Tom Lehrer once composed, saying 'If you don't love me

I'll kill myself', that he addressed to 'the occupier'. Cowardice is fatal to happiness (you die a thousand times), and the reason we are cowards is that the worst kind of pain is humiliation (the Nietzschean sneer from the unreliable audience at 'our worthiest hopes and goals'). As I've argued above, our conscience is no longer occupied by God or Morality, it is occupied by people, judges, and we in turn form the judging audience for others. So now we have to overcome the fact that this 'conscience dost make cowards of us all' if we are to be happy.

Bravery is the key to living with paradox in a particular sense. Because freedom and justification are paradoxically linked: they not only undermine, they redeem each other. The brave version of freedom is the one that is redeemed by having the courage to face the judgement of the audience. The brave version of justification is expressed through the need to be independent of those judgements.

	Anxious	**Brave**
Free	Escapist, Cynical, Mad	Self-reliant, Imaginative, Bold
Justified	Craven, Needy, Submissive	Trusting, Emotionally engaged

The *Brave* grouping is a dynamic interaction between freedom and justification that revolves around and around; this is how the happiness engine turns over. The *Anxious* grouping group splits apart. When the need to be justified is too anxious to stand up to the possibility of rejection or humiliation, it implodes into cravenness and submission; when the need to be free is too anxious to look back at a potent audience for approval it shears off into escapism, cynicism or madness. In searching for justification we must be brave enough to be free. In being free we must be brave enough to seek justification. Moreover, the words in the box above are *ascriptions* and depend ultimately, like a duck–rabbit, on the eye of the beholder. So the attempt to be brave, dependent as it is on unreliable audiences, is hazardous in itself.[22] When Yeats asked (implored, commanded, enjoined, begged, demanded? – the choice of words frames the answer) that his lover 'tread softly', was this an expression of bravery or anxiety? Was he craven or trusting? All we might say is that if it felt hard to say, it probably felt brave. If he couldn't help himself, it might just have been a bad, cringeworthy habit. You be the judge. All we can hope to do is to recognize and overcome our prevalent habits of self-protection in whichever direction they may lean. If we are tempted to run towards people, it might be brave to turn away; if we tend to run away, it might be brave to face them.

Moreover, bravery has nothing to do with fearlessness, nor in practice has it to do with heroism. Fear is necessary to bravery (only those with vertigo are brave when they look over the edge). In the context of this book, the fear I'm describing is the fear of humiliation; that the cheering we hope for from our audiences turns out to be jeering. The more extreme a risk you take of being jeered at and yet end up being cheered, the closer you are to being a hero. We all aspire to being heroes because only heroes are reliably happy. They can stand on the principle of being who they are and be sure to get adulation for it. Fully free and fully justified. The logic of happy endings co-opts this illusion. Jimmy Stewart's character in *It's a Wonderful Life* was a hero – he selflessly did what he thought was right irrespective of reward, and he paid a big price for it (lost his business, earned ridicule) and ended up with total vindication: the town sacrificed to save him *in extremis*. A hero never courts favour, but always ends up getting it, even if posthumously. Unfortunately, heroes and happy endings are a gilded figment of the Hollywood dream machine. In practice you can never be *assured* of favour unless you are submissive to some degree, acquire some technique – unless you are sufficiently cognizant of the norms that your audiences require. And quite right too: if you become impossible for your audience to judge you truly naked, you end up mad at least. To succeed you need to bend to the will of others, even though the most successful (the movie heroes) never bend. In reality the worst failures, the condemned, never bend either . . . or they bend too much.[23]

'It don't mean a thing if it ain't got that swing'

The problem with most Hollywood movies is that they can reinforce our sense of the comforting presence of reliable judges. They offer versions of life about which we needn't be anxious, because there is someone 'out there' who knows everything, whom we can count on. The omnipotent director and the omniscient audience are in cahoots to project true justification onto the characters. It doesn't matter that nobody in their lives notices Thelma and Louise driving off a cliff, or will ever know that they did so on purpose (killing themselves 'in their own fashion' as Freud requires) and with a smile. A sympathetic audience knows. We know. We will mourn them and feel for them and so justify them. The movie form plays a double trick on us: it turns us into gods while encouraging us to be children. We sit in the dark, omniscient and omnipresent in our knowing judgement of goodies and baddies while playing out our own infantile, silvered fantasies on the big screen long after the credits have rolled. Celebrities are the living proof that the movie never ends.

And here is where we must part company with Thelma and Louise and movies in general. If we want to live with paradox, we need to accept, intellectually, morally and emotionally that there is no ultimate, reliable audience watching us, and no such thing as happily ever after. We should give up on the ideals that movies tempt us to believe in. We can never be heroic or fearless in practice because that depends on having guaranteed applause, of being more sure than we can be that someone 'out there' knows what we are 'really' thinking. The fearless hero is the one who succeeds in making the audience too reliable. In the process, its judgement becomes impotent. Our audiences instead (at least the ones worth having) are fickle, biased, ill-informed and hard to please. We are anxious about their judgement (we can never count on it if it is to be worth more than canned laughter), and so we are stuck with merely trying to be brave and hoping to be judged well. In the *Boston Globe* debate concerning *Thelma and Louise*, Diane White commented on the women in the audience who

> cheered when Louise plugged the roadhouse cowboy who was trying to rape Thelma. And when the two characters blew up the rig of a leering, tongue-waggling trucker, they cheered even louder . . . [f]or some women 'Thelma and Louise' is a cathartic movie, a bit of wish fulfillment . . . I know what it's like to be so brutalized and humiliated by a man that you'd like to murder him. But I didn't. Why? Because life isn't a movie. Besides, unlike Louise, I didn't have a gun handy.

In this book I have tried to explain how and why happiness is so gripping and so elusive. I argue that we keep swinging between two competing needs, to *break free from* and to *embrace* other people. It is not simply that these needs contradict one another, they are literally paradoxical in that the successful expression of the one requires the assertion of its opposite. Happiness is not a destination or a formula; its pursuit has an inherently unstable dynamic that staggers between dreaming and accountability.

Aristotle identified magnanimity as a superlative virtue for a happy life, seeing it as the golden mean, the happy medium, between vanity and humility. *The Happiness Paradox* is an attempt to refute this fiction of 'a fine balance'. There is no *via media* between vanity (clothes shedding) and humility (clothes spreading), not least because the ascriptions of vanity or humility are not reliably achieved, even with good technique. If you draw a duck–rabbit badly it will tend to look more like one or the other. Draw it well and you do not get an average between the two; you get ambiguity. It depends on how you look at the picture: look too hard at the rabbit and you become aware of the duck. In the citations from Yeats and Garrison Keillor above, for example, we can see how humility might be a disguise for vanity. I am reminded of a remark made by the critic Clive James while reviewing the performance of another critic, Bernard Levin, on the television programme *Face the Music*. James noticed that every time Levin answered a question correctly he took a sip of water. For James that small action 'is supposed to look humble, but screams conceit'. Levin's technique isn't good enough for James – he wants to show a duck while James sees a rabbit. There is no space in which Levin can comfortably reside, safe in the knowledge that he's not too humble, not too vain. And in turn, when reading his line we must judge whether Clive James's technique is good enough for us: is his comment a display of acute perceptiveness and insight, or a petty and self-serving piece of point-scoring? The ascriptions of vanity and humility, as well as the Aristotelian average of magnanimity, are in the eye of the beholder. And the beholder, the potent audience, can cheer, jeer or sneer.

For the reasons I have outlined it is tempting to make static this dynamic swing and elevate one pole to obscure the other: to love freedom or defend justification. Yet freedom alone, through the fear of being trapped, can shear off into cynicism or alienation; justification alone through the fear of rejection can collapse into cravenness and submission. Either route, unredeemed by its opposite, is crippled by fear. And the only antidote to fear is *bravery*.

Bravery does not make you happy by itself, it is just a motor. It keeps the swing in motion. The commitment-phobe (like Louise's Jimmy) needs to be brave enough to commit, while a cowed submissive like Thelma needs to be brave enough to break away. This is hard enough: many people fail to shake off a bad habit or compulsion even after decades of analysis. Yet if they succeed in changing their character, and then get too comfortable in their new habits, the brave option will then be to head back in the direction they came from. Rather than clinging to one pole, or aiming for 'inner balance', the *pursuit* of happiness means endlessly swinging from disruption to conformity and back again; whether in the small scale of a specific conversation or in our lives as a whole; and then hoping to be judged well . . .

References

Introduction

1 Leo Tolstoy, *Anna Karenina*, trans. Richard Pevear and Larissa Volokonsky (Harmondsworth, 2001), pt. 1, chap. 1.
2 Aldous Huxley, 'Cynthia', from *Limbo: Six Stories and a Play* (London, 1975).
3 Coco Chanel in *Paris Review* (Spring 1956), p. 30.
4 From Philip Larkin, 'Born Yesterday', in *Collected Poems*, ed. Anthony Thwaite (New York, 1993).
5 George Santayana, *Life of Reason* (New York, 1998).
6 Walter Lippman, *Drift and Mastery* (Madison,WI, 1985), p. 100.
7 Quoted in Charles Guignon, *The Good Life* (Indianapolis, 1999), p. xi.

Chapter One: Happiness: A Brief History

1 From verse 50 of Whitman's *Song of Myself*, ed. Stephen Mitchell (Boston, MA, 1998).

2 Jonathan Freedman, *Happy People* (New York, 1980).

3 Bertrand Russell, *History of Western Philosophy* (London, 1984).

4 Bertrand Russell, *Marriage and Morals* (London, 1984).

5 Roy Porter, *Enlightenment* (Harmondsworth, 2001).

6 See, for example, Lewis and Haviland-Jones, *Handbook of Emotions* (2nd edn, New York, 2001).

7 Derek Edwards, *Discourse and Cognition* (London, 1996).

8 Clifford Geertz, *The Interpretation of Cultures* (London, 1973).

9 Quoted in Anthony O'Hear, *After Progress* (London, 1999).

10 Quoted in Deal Hudson, *Happiness and the Limits of Satisfaction* (Lanham, MD, 1995).

11 Michael Argyle, *The Psychology of Happiness* (London, 1987).

12 Hudson, *Happiness and the Limits of Satisfaction*.

13 From W. B. Yeats, 'Vacillation', in *The Winding Stair and other Poems* (1933).

Chapter Two: Feeling Free

1 Saul Bellow, *Ravelstein* (Harmondsworth, 2001).

2 For a wonderfully rich account of the development of modern identity see Charles Taylor, *Sources of the Self* (Cambridge, MA, 1989); a more accessible summary of his position is set out in Taylor, *Ethics of Authenticity* (Cambridge, MA, 1989).

3 Jean-Jacques Rousseau, 'Discourse on Inequality', in *The Social Contract and Discourses* (London, 1993).

4 *Schelling's Treatise on the Essence of Human Freedom*, trans. Martin Heidegger and Joan Stambaugh (Athens, OH, 1985).

5 Lippman, *Drift and Mastery*.

6 Robert Bellah et al., *Habits of the Heart* (Berkeley, CA, 1985), p. 284.

7 Quoted in Michael Billig, *Freudian Repression* (Cambridge, 1999), p. 213.

8 Charles Taylor, *Sources of the Self*, p. 511.

9 Charles Taylor, *Ethics of Authenticity*, p. 40.

10 Quoted in Charles Guignon, *The Good Life* (Indianapolis, 1999).

11 Richard Rorty, *Contingency, Irony and Solidarity* (Cambridge, 1989).

12 Henry David Thoreau, *Walden; or Life in the Woods* (Harmondsworth, 1984).

13 From Walt Whitman, 'Song of the Open Road', in *Leaves of Grass*, ed. Malcolm Cowley (Harmondsworth, 1979).

14 Ralph Waldo Emerson, *Self Reliance* (Toronto, 1993).

15 Lippman, *Drift and Mastery*, p. 103.

16 Vladimir Nabokov, *Lectures on Literature* (New York, 1980).

17 Quoted in Rorty, *Contingency*, p. 153.

18 When Skimpole, the child-like aesthete in *Bleak House*, causes the death of little Jo, Nabokov describes it as 'the false child betraying the real one'. What Nabokov does not countenance is that a real child can be just as cruel, that 'an evil man is a child grown strong'.

19 Rorty, *Contingency*, p. 165.

20 Rorty, *Contingency*, p. 159.

21 Friedrich Nietzsche, *The Gay Science* (Indianapolis, 1995).

22 He goes on to mock the socialist belief in a free society as a contradiction in terms, as built out of 'wooden iron' – as oxymoronic.

23 And to develop an aversion to 'big moral words and moral attitudes'.

24 Quoted in Guignon, *The Good Life*, p. 240.

25 Rorty, *Contingency*, p. 180.

26 Quoted in George Plimpton, ed., *Writers at Work: The Paris Review Interviews* (Paris, 1959).

27 Rorty, *Contingency*, p. 187.

28 Douglas Hofstadter, *Godel, Escher, Bach: An Eternal Golden Braid* (Harmondsworth, 1979).

29 Jacques Barzun, *Science: The Glorious Entertainment* (London, 1964).

30 Quoted in Adam Phillips, *Darwin's Worms* (London, 1999), p. 84.

31 Phillips, *Darwin's Worms*, p. 71.

32 In this context Phillips quotes Borges's line, 'Every man runs the risk of being the first immortal', and therefore the risk of being deprived of the ultimate means of escape.

33 Rorty, *Contingency*, p. 102.

34 Billig, *Freudian Repression*, p. 72.

35 Billig, *Freudian Repression*, p. 85.

36 Billig, *Freudian Repression*, p. 91.

37 Billig quotes Roland Barthes' observation that 'the said must be torn from the non-said'.

38 Billig, *Freudian Repression*, p. 76.

39 Ludwig Wittgenstein, *Culture and Value*, trans. Peter Winch, ed. G. H. von Wright (Chicago, 1984), p. 74e.

40 Tim Lott, *White City Blue* (Harmondsworth, 2000).

41 The philosopher Otto Neurath talks of the related difficulty of changing the deck on a ship – you always have to be standing on some of the planks in order to change the others.

42 Phillips, *Darwin's Worms*, p. 132.

43 Charles Taylor mentions as an example being the only person with 3,732 hairs on their head or being exactly the same height as some tree on the Siberian plain.

44 Bellah, *Habits of the Heart*, p. 84.

45 Max Frisch comments: 'We can now do what we want, and the only question is what do we want? At the end of our progress we stand where Adam and Eve once stood; and all we are faced with now is the moral question.' Quoted in Zygmunt Bauman, *Alone Again: Ethics after Uncertainty* (London, 1996).

46 From the 'Ethics of Ambiguity', in Guignon, *The Good Life*, pp. 268–9. De Beauvoir goes on to say: 'Only the freedom of others keeps each one of us from hardening in the absurdity of facticity.'

Chapter Three: Feeling Justified

1 Rom Harré, *Social Being* (Oxford, 1993), p. 32.

2 Sigmund Freud, 'Civilization and its Discontents', in *Civilization, Society and Religion* (Harmondsworth, 1985), p. 264.

3 The Israeli writer Amos Oz describes the family as the 'cradle of fanaticism'. The point for him is that, as with fanatics, parents are fundamentally

altruistic and want to change you for your own good!

4 Colin's stamp collecting later turned into computer programming and finally he turned to God.

5 Freud, 'Civilization and its Discontents', pp. 265–70.

6 He contrasts erotic with narcissistic character types. The erotic 'will give his first preference to his emotional relationships to other people', while the narcissistic man, who inclines to be self sufficient, will seek his main satisfactions in his internal mental processes'. 'Civilization and its Discontents', p. 272.

7 Though he is perfectly capable of a more abstract tone to make the following important theoretical point: 'Human nature is not a very human thing. By acquiring it, the person becomes a kind of construct, built up not from inner psychic propensities but from moral rules that are impressed on him from without. These rules, when followed, determine the evaluation he will make of himself and of his fellow-participants in the encounter, the distribution of his feelings, and the kinds of practices he will employ to maintain a specified and obligatory kind of ritual equilibrium. The general capacity to be bound by moral rules may well belong to the individual, but the particular set of rules which transforms him into a human being derives from requirements established in the ritual organization of social encounters'.

8 Erving Goffman, *The Presentation of Self in Everyday Life* (Harmondsworth, 1990), p. 62.

9 Goffman, *The Presentation of Self*, p. 87.

10 The audience can either confront and accuse or can become co-opted into the performance and look tactfully for ways to avoid stumbling backstage and spoiling the performance.

11 Or they may not be knowing enough and take your irony for sincerity and label you shallow.

12 *The Observer*, 5 March 2000.

13 William James, quoted in Goffman, *The Presentation of Self*, p. 57.

14 A true athlete may love the adulation that comes from success but largely pursues some more abstract dream. My friend Blaise used to run and was driven by the mantra 'the stopwatch doesn't care about your ego', and my

brother Leith, a discus-thrower, pursues the dream of throwing a discus so far they will have to rebuild stadia.

15 From *The Guardian, Weekend*, 27 May 2000. Sontag is described as having 'in abundance two qualities, *courage and conscience*. No false gods now'. (emphasis added).

16 George Eliot, *Middlemarch* (Oxford, 1998), p. 282.

17 To achieve 'closure', as the gurus call it, means the person no longer has power over you and is no longer in your audience. We are ourselves powerful in the eyes of others, we form their audience, and intimacy comes from walking a tightrope between having power and conceding it.

18 Rom Harré in *Social Being* describes this using the concept of 'character': 'An essential element in the understanding of the social activities of human beings derives from their attribution to each other of permanent moral qualities. I have called this attribution "character". It is made of the attributes that a particular group of people ascribe to an individual on the basis of the impressions they have formed of him on the basis of his expressive activities. These attributes, or rather the beliefs that people have as to those attributes, determine the expectations that a group forms of a person. They are the foundations, as individual beliefs of the willingness of others to defer to and praise an individual or to denigrate him, or simply ignore him. They are the ultimate basis of his moral career.'

19 Richard Rorty, in *Essays on Heidegger and Others* (Cambridge, 1991), points out that 'the appearance of paradox results from the fact that "morality" can mean either the attempt to be just in one's treatment of others (the [Eudaemonistic] version studied fruitlessly by moral philosophy since the Greeks) or the search for perfection in oneself. The former is public morality, codifiable in statutes and maxims. The latter is private morality, the development of character' (p. 153).

20 Rorty, *Essays on Heidegger and Others*, p. 154.

21 Annette Baier, in *A Progress of Sentiments* (Cambridge, MA, 1991), comments that 'jealousy of character is the acid test. As Hume puts it . . . The test is not "What qualities would I wish to have?" but "What qualities would I wish my fellows to find in me?" (p. 199).

22 Richard Sennett, *The Corrosion of Character* (New York, 1998), pp. 145–6.

23 Except when they can flay our intimacy by using a publicly visible vulnerability and stigma – which are widespread in a world where 'In an important sense there is only one complete unblushing male in America: a young, married, white, urban, northern, heterosexual Protestant father of college education, fully employed, of good complexion, weight, and height, and a recent record in sports . . . Any male who fails to qualify in any of these ways is likely to view himself – during moments at least – as unworthy, incomplete, and inferior.' From Erving Goffman, *Stigma* (Harmondsworth, 1963), p. 128.

24 Adam Phillips, *Monogamy* (London, 1996), aphorism no. 7.

25 Rorty, *Contingency*, p. 179.

26 Emmanuel Levinas, *Otherwise than Being* (Dordrecht, 1998), pp. 48–9. 'Saying uncovers the one that speaks . . . The unblocking of communication . . . is accomplished in saying . . . It is in the risky uncovering of oneself, in sincerity, the breaking up of inwardness and the abandon of all shelter, exposure to traumas, vulnerability.'

27 Quoted in Charles Lemert and Ann Branaman, *The Goffman Reader* (Oxford, 1997), p. LIII.

28 Lemert and Branaman, *The Goffman Reader*, p. lxi.

29 William Shakespeare, *Hamlet*, act III, scene i.

30 Ironically, the arch-theorist of freedom, Nietzsche, tells us what is needed to be truly justified. For Nietzsche we can only give from a position of strength, so to be capable of selfishness is critical to being generous since this is the only guarantee that it results from a free decision rather than through convention.

31 Goffman, *The Presentation of Self*, p. 206.

32 Goffman, *The Presentation of Self*, p. 236.

Chapter Four: Love

1 Quoted in A. C. Grayling, *The Quarrel of the Age: The Life and Times of William*

Hazlitt (London, 2000).

2 Francesco Alberoni, 'Falling in Love', full text available at
   http://www.alberoni.it/frfallingeng.html

3 Zygmunt Bauman, 'On the Postmodern Uses of Sex', in Mike Featherstone,
   ed., *Love and Eroticism* (London, 1999).

4 Charles Lindholm, 'Love and Structure', reprinted in Featherstone, *Love and
   Eroticism*.

5 Steven Pinker, *How the Mind Works* (New York, 1997), p. 417.

6 Pinker, *How the Mind Works*, p. 419.

7 Mary Evans, 'Falling in Love with Love is Falling for Make Believe: Ideologies
   of Romance in Post-Enlightenment Culture', reprinted in Featherstone,
   Love and Eroticism.

8 Jane Austen, *Pride and Prejudice* (Harmondsworth, 1994), p. 375.

9 Quoted in Charles Lindholm, 'Love and Structure' reprinted in Featherstone,
   Love and Eroticism, p. 245.

10 Lindholm describes how the ideal of the love match is also seen in small-
   scale hunter-gathering cultures like the Ife of Central Africa, the Kung
   bushmen of Botswana and the Ojibway of North America's Great Lakes
   region. These cultures (like Western society) also prize individualism, are
   highly mobile, with little attachment to kin groups – as free agents who
   choose whom they marry, they also tend to describe their motives as based
   on true love.

11 Umberto Eco, '1985: 17 Reflections on "The Name of the Rose"', *Encounter*,
   64(4) 1985, pp. 7–19.

12 Dorothy Tennov, *Limerence* (Tea Gardens, NSW, 1987). reprinted by
   Scarborough House in 1999 (*Love and Limerence: The Experience of Being in
   Love*).

13 Jean-Paul Sartre, *Being and Nothingness* (London, 1998), p. 367. The lover 'wishes
   that the Other's freedom should determine itself to become love – and this
   not only at the beginning of the affair but at each instant – and at the same
   time he wants this freedom to be captured by itself, to turn back on itself, as
   in madness, as in a dream, so as to will its own captivity. This captivity must
   be a resignation that is both free and yet chained in our hands.'

14 We may convince ourselves otherwise, that true independence has nothing to do with impression management, but the truly independent as I argued in chapter Two is either mad or dead. The truly independent wouldn't have the slightest objection to being thought craven or abject in front of their potent audiences.

15 'Unfortunate Coincidence' by Dorothy Parker.

16 From Ulrich Beck and Elisabeth Beck-Gernsheim, *The Normal Chaos of Love* (Oxford, 1995), p. 11.

17 Phillips, *Monogamy*, aphorism no. 28.

18 Erica Jong, quoted in Beck and Beck-Gersheim, *The Normal Chaos of Love*.

19 Quoted in Robert Skidelsky, *John Maynard Keynes: The Economist as Saviour, 1920–1937* (London, 1992), p. xvii.

20 Quoted in Pinker, *How the Mind Works*, p. 483.

21 Sigmund Freud, *Sexuality and the Psychology of Love* (New York, 1963), p. 40.

22 Phillips, *Monogamy*, no. 11.

23 Phillips, *Monogamy*, no. 62.

24 Phillips, *Monogamy*, no. 70.

25 Phillips, *Monogamy*, no. 84.

26 Beck and Beck-Gersheim, *The Normal Chaos of Love*, p. 198.

27 C. S. Lewis, *A Grief Observed* (London, 1966), p. x.

28 Robert Bellah, *Habits of the Heart*, p. 70.

29 Pablo Neruda, 'Sonnet XVII', in Robert Hass and Stephen Mitchell, eds, *Into the Garden* (New York, 1993).

30 Quoted in Jonathan Dollimore, *Death, Desire and Loss in Western Culture* (Harmondsworth, 1998), p. 314.

31 From 'Lullaby' by W. H. Auden, in *Selected Poems*, ed. Edward Mendelson (London, 1979), p. 50.

32 Dollimore, *Death, Desire and Loss in Western Culture*.

33 Martha Nussbaum, *Love's Knowledge: Essays on Philosophy and Literature* (New York, 1992).

34 Charles Dickens, *David Copperfield* (London, 1991), p. 345.

35 Nussbaum poses the question: 'Why is it that, morally attuned as the reader of this novel is made to be, the reader nonetheless falls in love, as David

also falls in love, with James Steerforth? Why, and how, does this novel, which begins with an open question about who the hero of David Copperfield's life actually is, and which ends (apparently) with the upward-pointing gesture of morality [marriage to Agnes], lead us at times, outside of morality into the "shadowy world" of moonlight and love, of magic, and an arm curved along the pillow?'.

And answers it with: 'David's movement from morality to Steerforth, and his refusal to judge the person he loves, are, then, motivated not only by romantic desire, but by a complex attitude in which desire is linked with active loyalty and support, fantasy with the true perception of the particular . . . If Agnes . . . represents wisdom . . . David's love emerges as the love that is "better and stronger than wisdom." If Agnes is the judicious spectator, he is as mobile participant, stronger than the spectator. His very susceptibility to extramoral danger [to Steerforth] is part of his strength, and part of the strength of his love.'

36 From 'Love' by Philip Larkin.

Chapter Five: Work

1 Ray Pahl, *After Success* (Oxford, 1995), p. 54.

2 From Philip Larkin, *Toads* (1955).

3 Billig, *Freudian Repression*, p. 257.

4. Fyodor Dostoevsky, *Memoirs from The House of the Dead* (Oxford, 2001). It should be pointed out that in the same novel he also says that if you want to crush a person's spirit, just give them work that is completely meaningless and irrational. 'If he had to move a heap of earth from one place to another and back again – I believe the convict would hang himself . . . preferring rather to die than endure . . . such humiliation, shame and torture'.

5 By contrast, the transactional quality underlying our experience of love must remain hidden, as I argued in chapter Four.

6 See Stephen Lea, et al., *The Individual in the Economy* (Cambridge, 1987).

7   From Adam Smith, *The Wealth of Nations*, quoted in Paul Strathern, *Dr Strangelove's Game* (Harmondsworth, 2002), p. 109.

8   Karl Marx and Friedrich Engels, *The Communist Manifesto* (Oxford, 1998) and 1848.

9   He also doubled his workers' pay to $5 per day, ostensibly to enable them to buy the cars they made, but in practice (according to Zygmunt Bauman) this was essential to keeping the staff he had trained to such perfection. As economist J. K. Galbraith observed, 'clearly the most unfortunate people are those who must do the same thing over and over again, every minute, or perhaps twenty to the minute. They deserve the shortest hours and the highest pay.'

10 Apparently the data didn't strongly support the conclusion (see S.E.A. Lea, et al., *The Individual in the Economy*, New York, 1987, p. 168), but the important point the historical moment in which these studies were used to usher in a new way to think of motivation at work known today as the 'human relations' movement.

11 See Chris Argyris, for example, who contrasts the Bureaucratic/Pyramidal with the Humanistic/Democratic value systems played out in organizations.

12 Richard Sennett, *The Corrosion of Character* (New York, 1998), p. 30.

13 The sociologist Robert Bellah in another piece of cultural diagnosis, *Habits of the Heart*, describes Brian who has found, like Rico, 'the high road to corporate success has led [him] back and forth across the country, "picking up, selling the house, moving off to a strange city and strange state" every few years, making new friends and then leaving them behind again' (p. 68).

14 Joshua Halberstam, *Work: Making and Living Making a Life* (Berkeley, California, 2000).

15 Sennett, *The Corrosion of Character*.

16 Sennett, *The Corrosion of Character*, p. 109.

17 Sennett, *The Corrosion of Character*, p. 112.

18 Gideon Kunda, quoted in Sennett, p. 112.

19 Sennett, *The Corrosion of Character*, p. 112.

20 Erving Goffman, *The Presentation of Self in Everyday Life* (Harmondsworth, 1990), p. 108.

21 See Sennett's chapter in Will Hutton and Anthony Giddens, *On the Edge* (New York, 2001), p. 188.

22 Alasdair Macintyre, *After Virtue* (London, 1981), p. 30.

23 Excerpts from *The Office* are taken from Ricky Gervais and Steve Merchant, *The Office: The Scripts* (London, 2002).

24. See, for example, Craig R. Hichman, *Mind of a Manager, Soul of a Leader* (Chichester, 1990).

25 'Breakthrough Leadership, It's Personal', *Harvard Business Review* (December 2001).

26 'Breakthrough Leadership, It's Personal', p. 8.

27 Taken from Ford Company website, 22 November 2002, URL http://www.ford.com/en/ourCompany/corporateCitizenship/ ourLearningJourney/messageFromTheChairman.htm

28 Quoted in David Schoenbrun, *The Three Lives of Charles de Gaulle*, Atheneum 66.

29 Various models emphasize the individual or the context, and there are some that emphasize both, e.g., Fielder's *Contingency Model*. But very few see these aspects truly interacting.

30 Haslam uses self-categorization theory (an offshoot of Social Identity Theory) to show that our levels of motivation (*à la* Maslow) are crucially dependent on 'self-category salience'. That is to say when I define myself socially (through shared group membership) I will be motivated by justification and will be loyal to group norms, whereas when I define myself individually (personal identity) I am going to express my need to be free. He cites conditions under which each of these self-categorizations may become salient.

31 Alex Haslam, *Psychology in Organizations* (London, 2001), p. 105.

32 The phrase is taken from Steve Reicher and Nick Hopkins, *Self and Nation* (London, 2001), who are writing in the context of political leadership. They argue 'that leadership tends not to alight upon an individual but is actively sought. The practice of leadership is about the strategic creation of

personal and collective realities so as to merge the two (or separate them in the case of one's rivals).

33 Haslam, *Psychology in Organizations*.

34 My friend and colleague Karen Phillips offered a nice illustration of this in the context of parenting. It is no good *feeling* love for your child, if the child doesn't experience it. You have to *perform* love – even if that means running against your other principles of integrity and honesty. 'That's a really wonderful painting' you say to your three year old who has more zeal than skill.

35 The beauty of the fly on the wall genre is that it conveys the idea that we are watching those who do not know they are being watched – we see their Hobbesian 'state of nature'. We are of course watching excellent actors performing as inadequate actors. Alan Partridge, the character created by Steve Coogan, provides another uncomfortable yet compelling spectacle for the same reasons.

36 He is drawing here on Richard Rorty's language in *Contingency, Solidarity and Irony*.

37 Sennett, *Corrosion of Character*, pp. 115–16. Sennett puts the mechanism more formally thus: 'An authority figure is someone who takes responsibility for the power that he or she wields. In an old-style work hierarchy, the boss might do that by overtly declaring, "I have the power, I know what's best, obey me". Modern management techniques seek to escape from the authoritarian aspects of such declarations, but in the process they manage to escape as well from being held responsible for their acts . . . If "change" is the responsible agent, if everybody is a "victim", then authority vanishes, for no one can be held accountable – certainly not this manager letting people go' (p. 114).

38 Richard Scase, 'Why We're so Clockwise', *The Observer*, 26 August 2001.

39 '"We don't trust the boss" say British Workers': 6–9 November 1998. From MORI website.

40 While these topics are respectively about the 'why' and the 'what' of trust, D. H. McKnight, L. L. Cummings & N. L. Chervany, 'Initial Trust Formation in New Organizational Relationships', *Academy of Management Review*, 23:3

(1998), pp. 473–90, show that there is a lack of deep study on the dynamic development of trust: its 'how'. They state: 'Trust has usually been studied as a static, rather than dynamic, variable' (p. 5).

41 Robert Wuthnow concluded from his thorough empirical research about trust based on survey data: 'For most people, trust is not simply a matter of making rational calculations about the possibility of benefiting by cooperating with someone else. Social scientists who reduce the study of trust to questions about rational choice, and who argue that it has nothing to do with moral discourse, miss that point' (Wuthnow 1998 quoted in Bo Rothstein, 'Trust, Social Dilemmas and Collective Memories', in *Journal of Theoretical Politics*, XIV/4 (October 2000).

42 If you search on Google with the key words 'decision making' and 'uncertainty', you can begin to see how much energy people can place in trying to solve the insoluble.

43 The point is reinforced in a broader context by Onora O'Neill in her 2002 Reith Lectures: 'Our revolution in accountability has not reduced attitudes of mistrust, but rather reinforced a culture of suspicion. Instead of working towards intelligent accountability based on good governance, independent inspection and careful reporting, we are galloping towards central planning by performance indicators, reinforced by obsessions with blame and compensation. This is pretty miserable both for those who feel suspicious and for those who are suspected of untrustworthy action – sometimes with little evidence'.

44. Jessica Miller, 'Trust: The Moral Importance of an Emotional Attitude', in the journal *Practical Philosophy* (November, 2000). She goes on to point out that 'this feature of trust is overlooked in accounts which view trust solely as a response to prior actions of the trusted. Trust is a forward-looking phenomenon, in that my perception of the trusted leads me to interpret her actions and intentions as benevolent.'

45 Annette Baier, 'Trust and Antitrust', *Ethics*, 96 (January 1986), pp. 231–60; pp. 234–5.

46 From Jean-Paul Sartre, *Being and Nothingness*, quoted in Erving Goffman, *The Presentation of Self in Everyday Life* (Harmondsworth, 1990), p. 42.

Chapter Six: Living with Paradox

1 In case you need to know, P stands for Personal Characteristics, including outlook on life, adaptability and resilience. E stands for Existence and relates to health, financial stability and friendships. And H represents Higher Order needs, and covers self-esteem, expectations, ambitions and sense of humour.

2 Will Ferguson, *Happiness*^{TM} (Edinburgh, 2002).

3 Since we literally see the world through a spectrum of colour and so powerful is the visual metaphor in our language (seeing is believing), that we easily place our concepts on imaginary spectra too.

4. First conceived by the Gestalt psychologist J. Jastrow in 1900 and later used by Wittgenstein. See Ludwig Wittgenstein, *Philosophical Investigations*, 3rd edn, trans. G.E.M. Anscombe (New York, 1967), pp. 193–6.

5 Sartre, who sees us as 'condemned to be free' opposes *facticity* (our rootedness in the everyday world, in our bodies and our social context – stones in the fabric) with *transcendence* (our yearning to escape the bonds of reality). For Sartre 'bad faith' or self-deception comes out of a denial either of 'facticity' (which we do when we claim we are free unencumbered spirits) or 'transcendence' (when claiming we are stuck in the world as we find it without hope of change). What we must do, he claims, is 'affirm facticity as *being* transcendence and transcendence as *being* facticity, in such a way that at the instant when a person apprehends the one, he can find himself abruptly faced with the other'.

6 Friedrich Nietzsche, *On the Advantage and Disadvantage of History for Life*, trans. Peter Preuss (Indianapolis, 1980).

7 Nietzsche distinguished between those with a master morality that is purified of all self-interest, since the master already has power, and the slave morality of the powerless that is self-seeking. I would go further and say we are *both* masters and slaves (actors and stones) – as masters we express our need for freedom and as slaves our need for justification. The paradox comes from the fact that in our assertion of mastery we must reassert our slavery, and our slave morality leads directly back to mastery.

8 The philosopher Alasdair Macintyre frames the issue well in *After Virtue* (London, 1981), p. 308. Macintyre would take issue with my version since he places great moral weight on the reified concept of tradition and universal goods. His 'community' has rather more ontological or moral weight than my audience.

9 To some viewers, *Thelma and Louise* appears to be no more than the female version of *Butch Cassidy and the Sundance Kid*, a 'male buddy movie'. To others, it's meaningless, insignificant, and a 'fraud', and, 'if we see significance [in it] where none exists, any debate that ensues likely will be irrelevant.' But the debate that *did* ensue included widely differing conclusions about the movie. See, for example, Shirley A. Wiegand, 'Deception and Artifice: Thelma, Louise and the Legal Hemeneutic', *Oklahoma City University Law Review*, XXII/1 (1997).

10 Quoted in Elizabeth V. Spelman and Martha Minow, 'Outlaw Women: An Essay on *Thelma & Louise*', 26 *New England Law Review* 1281 (1992).

11 The dialogue, as well as the parenthetical asides, are taken from Callie Khouri's final shooting script, 5 June 1990. The whole script can be found at http://www.hundland.com/scripts/ThelmaAndLouise.txt

12 Recall the discussion in chapter Three on how Sartre and Freud both saw death as a way to foil biographers who wanted to trap their vivid lives in borrowed words.

13 It wouldn't have worked for an individual suicide. Like Butch and Sundance, Bonnie and Clyde, there is great solidarity in facing the end together.

14. This is not to suggest that habits are easily changed.

15 Richard Rorty, *Truth and Progress* (Cambridge, 1998), pp. 48–9.

16 From William Shakespeare, *Hamlet*, act I, scene iii.

17 Steve Reicher, unpublished manuscript.

18 Thomas Hardy, *Tess of the D'Urbervilles* (Harmondsworth, 1978), p. 486.

19 Anxiety is essentially fear that has lost its object through unconsciously formed emotive tensions that express 'internal dangers' rather than externalised threats. Anthony Giddens, *Modernity and Self-identity: Self and Society in the Late Modern Age* (Cambridge, 1991), p. 44.

20 Garrison Keillor, *Lake Wobegone Days* (London 1986).

21 Jean-Paul Sartre, *Being and Nothingness* (London, 1969), p. 248.

22 Rom Harré, *Social Being* (Oxford 1993), p. 30. comments that 'human life is sufficiently complex, at least in modern society, for someone to interact with several non-overlapping sets of others, and perhaps to *acquire several characters*. Public social reputation can be sought, risked, gained or lost in public, in the course of those conventional trials I have called hazards . . . But the existence of hazards and of the institutions for the giving and marking of respect and contempt allow for the possibility of a downward moral career through failure at hazard. Failure is defined reciprocally to the success from which one gains respect and dignity, and it is marked by humiliation. The experience of humiliation is the reciprocal of the maintenance of dignity.

23 Bravery is about replacing a present audience with a distant one. We can't justify ourselves to objective standards but only to real or imagined or future audiences. As expressed in the notorious line 'I was just following orders' we have enormous pressure from the majority through peer group pressure. So since we can't call upon the God's-eye point of view to do the heroic thing we need to be mad (free) enough to hear the views of an imagined or future audience as louder than the roar in your ears of the present one.

Acknowledgements

I started writing this book when my daughter Anna was born. She appears briefly in chapter Two as a two year old and is now four. In that time I've been grateful for the advice, support, encouragement and, above all, patience of friends, family and colleagues who've long endured my enthusiasm for this theme.

My thanks go to David McCune for encouragement from the start as well as to Stephen Clark and Louise Murray, who also read and commented acutely on early drafts.

I must thank Rom Harré, David Hill, Leith Marar, David Owen, Lucy Robinson, Dirk Snelders, Sandra Tharumalingam and Dominique Woodward, all of whom read and commented thoughtfully and helpfully on parts of the manuscript, as well as Tracey Ozmina, who provided a key set of references for chapter Four. Peter Hamilton was an engaged, constructive and encouraging series editor.

I'm indebted to Geoff Lattimer, who provided helpful advice and valuable commentary throughout the writing process. Thanks also to Robert Rojek, who never read any of it, but whose conversation has coloured every chapter, and special thanks are due to Kiren Shoman, Julian Lewis and my father, Nael Marar, all of whom read and commented extensively on the entire manuscript (including revisions) with generosity, knowledge and care. I learned a lot, and happily take full responsibility for the failings that remain.

This last year has been particularly rewarding and deadline-threatening thanks to the arrival of Anna's sisters, Ellie and Charlotte. For that reason, among so many, I am grateful above all to their mother, Kate Buchanan, whose love, sheer strength, critical feedback and ever-potent gaze have sustained me through the whole project.

All chapter opening illustrations are wood-engravings by the celebrated Thomas Bewick (1753–1828).